Voyages and Adventures of La Pérouse

Voyages and

From the fourteenth edition of the

F. Valentin abridgment, Tours, 1875

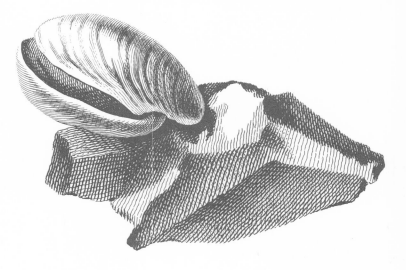

Adventures
of La Pérouse

Translated from the French by Julius S. Gassner

Lapérouse

HONOLULU: UNIVERSITY OF HAWAII PRESS: 1969

PUBLISHED FOR FRIENDS OF THE LIBRARY OF HAWAII

COPYRIGHT 1969 UNIVERSITY OF HAWAII PRESS

Manufactured in the United States of America

LIBRARY OF CONGRESS CATALOG CARD NO. 68-13887

STANDARD BOOK NUMBER 87022-445-X

" Many the wonders but nothing walks stranger than man.
This thing crosses the sea in the winter's storm,
making his path through the roaring waves."

SOPHOCLES

JOHN FRANCIS GALAUP
DE LA PÉROUSE,
Commodore in the French Navy, born at Alby in 1741.

TRANSLATOR'S PREFACE

THIS TRANSLATION of an abridged version of La Pérouse's report of his "Voyage Around the World" has been made in the belief that the fame of Admiral Jean-François Galaup, Comte de La Pérouse, has been unduly eclipsed by that of Captain James Cook, R.N. As Pacific explorer par excellence, Cook rightly deserves to head the list of the eighteenth-century explorers who corrected the errors of their predecessors and filled in the many blank spaces on the map of the Pacific Ocean. Cook's career has been the subject of numerous books in English, and in the various historical works and text books considerable attention has been given to his accomplishments.

Second only to Cook, and the foremost French explorer of the Pacific in the eighteenth century, La Pérouse is virtually unknown in the United States outside of esoteric circles.[1] Almost completely ignored by American writers in the nineteenth century, he received little notice until 1959, when two works dealing with his expedition were published.[2] The same hiatus exists in our general periodical literature.

---

[1] See Percy Sykes, *A History of Exploration* (New York: Harper Bros., 1961), which contains a chapter on Cook and a paragraph on La Pérouse.

[2] Charles N. Rudkin, *The First French Expedition to California*: *La Pérouse in 1786* (Los Angeles: Glen Dawson, 1959); Edward Weber Allen, *The Vanishing Frenchman: The Mysterious Disappearance of Lapérouse* (Rutland, Vt.: C. E. Tuttle, Co., 1959).

This indifference can be explained partly by the fact that the expedition of La Pérouse was terminated the year before the French Revolution began. The search for La Pérouse which was conducted by d'Entrecasteaux ended in the same year which saw the start of the War of the First Coalition. The official publication of the report of La Pérouse's voyage appeared in 1797, shortly before the War of the Second Coalition. World conditions at the time of the French Revolution and Napoleon were not conducive to spreading the fame of La Pérouse in the English-speaking world.

Furthermore, even if those years had been peaceful, the mere fact that the original reports and most of the subsequent literature on La Pérouse were in the French language militated against the spread of La Pérouse's reputation in the United States. Combine the linguistic factor with the natural long-term cultural orientation of the United States toward English history and literature rather than to the French, and we have gone a long way toward explaining why Cook has all but monopolized the pages which tell of the exploration of the Pacific in the eighteenth century.

Nevertheless, a number of English editions of La Pérouse's reports have been published; most of them made their appearance shortly after the French edition was first published in 1797. There was at least one American edition, an abridgment issued in 1801.[3]

The title of the original French edition, *Voyage de La Pérouse autour du Monde*, is misleading since La Pérouse did not circumnavigate the world. Rather, he sailed the length and breadth of the Pacific, crossing it from south to north, from east to west, and again from north to south. In the course of his travels, he stopped at Chile, Alaska, California, Macao, Manila, Siberia, Sakhalin Island, Kamchatka, and Australia, as well as at numerous islands in Oceania.

The purpose of the expedition, which was sent out by the government of Louis XVI, was the advancement of science and the promotion of French foreign trade. In carrying out the first of these objectives, La Pérouse sent

---

[3] *A Voyage Round the World, Performed in the Years 1785, 1786, 1787, 1788, by M. de la Pérouse: Abridged from the Original French Journal . . .* Boston, printed for Joseph Bumstead, 1801.

back to Europe the most comprehensive description to date of Sakhalin Island and the Siberian coast opposite it. His principal discovery was of the strait which separates Sakhalin Island and Hokkaido and connects the Sea of Japan with the southern part of the Okhotsk Sea. His reports include detailed, accurate observations of the natives of Siberia, Sakhalin Island, Alaska, and Oceania, thereby providing stimulating material for the newly developing science of anthropology. The scientists who accompanied him gathered data which promoted all of the natural sciences, particularly astronomy, botany, geography, geology, meteorology, oceanography, and zoology. The expedition had the opportunity to correct and supplement various observations made by Captain Cook's party a few years earlier.

Although the climate and natural beauty of some of the islands of Oceania impressed the expedition so favorably that they were described as a paradise, La Pérouse did not subscribe to the myth of the "noble savage" popular in the French Enlightenment. Rather, his reports helped to dispel the romantic fallacy which had beguiled such sedentary intellectuals as Diderot and Rousseau. In his humane attitude toward the natives, however, La Pérouse exemplified one of the better trends of the Enlightenment.

La Pérouse's reports are of interest not only to specialists in the history of eighteenth-century France and the exploration of the Pacific, but also to general readers in the United States. The attention of the American public has been increasingly turned toward the Pacific and westward across its vast expanses to the shores of the Far East. Since 1784, when the *Empress of China* first sailed from Boston to Canton, until the latest arrival of a tourist-laden luxury liner at Suva, from the first colonization of Hawaii by New England missionaries in 1820 to the assignment of Micronesia to the United States as a strategic trusteeship, the Pacific has played an increasingly greater role in the lives of Americans. This trend has been accompanied by a corresponding growth of Pacific studies and literature, in which, it is believed, the epic of La Pérouse deserves a more prominent place.

As stated above, the original report of La Pérouse's expedition was first published in Paris in 1797. The three volumes of this edition were condensed into one small volume by F. Valentin in about 1840 and published by Alfred Mame and Sons, Tours. In producing a more readable version of the original report, Valentin omitted technical data, shortened the descriptive passages, and changed the narrative from the first person to the third. The present translation is of the fourteenth edition of Valentin's abridgment, which was published in 1875 and includes a supplement consisting of notes from the journal of Dr. Rollin, ship's surgeon, and an appendix describing the efforts made to solve the mystery of the disappearance of La Pérouse's expedition.

The questions of nomenclature, to quote J. C. Beaglehole, are somewhat troublesome. Some of the places visited by La Pérouse, in particular the islands, no longer have the names by which they were known to eighteenth-century Europeans. Each of the various European nations had the habit of giving a different name to the same place, usually out of national pride. This translation retains the original place names used by La Pérouse, and where these are substantially different from the present ones, the modern equivalent has been inserted in brackets immediately following the first mention of the name.

Footnotes marked Valentin are those of the French abridgment. All other footnotes are mine.

I wish to express my gratitude to Dr. Harold E. Davis, my colleague at the University of Albuquerque, for reading the manuscript of the translation and for recommending a number of necessary changes, and to my wife for constant aid and advice in producing a version which may be a source of pleasure as well as information.

JULIUS S. GASSNER
Albuquerque, New Mexico, 1969

CONTENTS

ILLUSTRATIONS

All illustrations, including the drawings of sea creatures and insects reproduced as decorations throughout the book, are from the engravings published with the original account of the La Pérouse expedition, Paris 1797.

INTRODUCTION

THE UNKNOWN exercises a mysterious power over our minds. If one of the unfortunate companions of La Pérouse had escaped from the wreck of the two ships commanded by the illustrious navigator and had returned home to tell us that both crews had perished on a nameless rock in the Pacific Ocean, every sensitive heart would certainly have been filled with sorrow, but that would have been the end of the story, and today the captain would hardly be any more famous than any other of the great number of brave sea-farers who, like him, sought glory by discovering far-off, unknown countries. Such was not the fate of La Pérouse. In the midst of his distant and dangerous travels, he suddenly disappeared and in doing so he left the world a mystery to unravel. For more than forty years, like a mother seeking news of her soldier son from all who were returning from the theater of war, France questioned the various European navigators to learn if they had come across some trace of La Pérouse and his companions. Was he still alive in some unexplored wilderness, without the hope of ever returning home? Was he the wretched slave of some savage nation? Such were the questions that were asked.

The man who excited the sympathy of the nation to so high a degree was Rear Admiral Jean-François Galaup, Comte de La Pérouse. Born at Albi in 1741, he entered the Naval Academy at an early age. There he was fired by the example of navigators who had glorified their country, and there he resolved to follow their course. Appointed a midshipman on November 19, 1756, he participated in eight campaigns against the English. He distinguished himself on several occasions, and his youthful merit began to attract the attention of his superiors.

On October 1, 1764, he was promoted to the rank of ensign. From that date until 1780, few officers had a more active career than he. He engaged in several actions, contributed to the success of more than one battle, and captured several warships from the English. Commissioned a captain on April 11, 1780, he was in command of the frigate *Astrée* when on July 2, while cruising with the *Hermione*, he joined in a stubborn battle with six English ships of the line [1] near Cape North, Cape Breton Island, off the coast of Canada. Five of these ships lined up to wait for him while the sixth remained beyond the range of his cannon. Under full sail, the two French frigates attacked the enemy. They maneuvered so skillfully that the English squadron was soon in a state of confusion. At the end of a half hour, two of the five ships were forced to surrender; the other three would have suffered the same fate if nightfall had not rescued them from the pursuit.

In 1781, the French government developed a plan to seize and destroy the British bases on Hudson Bay. La Pérouse seemed to be the right man to carry out a mission in such dangerous waters. He sailed from Cape Frances, Haiti [Dominican Republic], with a squadron composed of the *Sceptre*, seventy-four guns, the frigates *Astrée* and *Engageante*, thirty-six guns each, carrying on board two hundred fifty infantrymen, forty artillerymen, four pieces of field artillery, two mortars, and three hundred rounds of ammunition. The weather that year, even during the summer, was exceptionally severe just below the polar circle. La Pérouse had hardly made twenty-five leagues into Hudson Strait when he found the bay frozen. All around were huge floes, thick fogs, and frequent snowstorms blown down from the pole. In the face of these obstacles, he exercised outstanding leadership and the greatest navigational skill. Overcoming the opposition of the elements, he accomplished his mission by completely destroying Fort Prince of Wales and Fort York, both of which belonged to the Hudson

---

[1] The largest warship, known as a "ship of the line," mounted from 60 to 120 guns.

Bay Company. Although by destroying the property of the enemy he carried out the stern orders which he had received, he was not unmindful of their personal misfortune. Informed that at his approach a number of the English had fled into the forest where they ran the risk of death by starvation or of capture by the savages, he generously left them with a supply of food and arms when he departed. Distinguished as he was as a soldier and a navigator, this act of humanity shows he was even more outstanding for his personal qualities. Full of the vitality characteristic of Mediterranean people, he was as pleasant in his relations with his subordinates as with his equals. His personality sparkled with charm and wit. The English who had tested him in battle did not hesitate to recognize his excellence; for his part, he spoke only with respect of the immortal Captain Cook and always acknowledged the achievements of the great men of other nations who had followed the same career as he.

A short time after La Pérouse had returned to France, where his reputation as a skilled navigator was by then firmly established, the government decided to take advantage of the peace which had just been concluded with England and to assume its responsibilities as a first-class naval power and more especially as one dedicated to the advancement of science by sending out a scientific expedition. King Louis XVI, who wished to promote the glory and advantage of his people and who had an extensive knowledge of geography, joined Fleurieu,[2] the scientist and a friend of La Pérouse, in outlining the course of the expedition. Its purpose was to discover new lands and to establish commercial relations with them; to collect precise data on whaling in the waters off South America and the Cape of Good Hope and on the fur trade between North America and China and even Japan; finally, to make a careful reconnaissance of the northwest coast of North America, Japanese waters, the Solomon Islands, and the southwest coast of Australia. Since the proper accomplishment of such a mission required superior leadership, the choice fell upon La Pérouse. More than anyone else, he was capable of directing a long and dangerous voyage through unknown seas off shores inhabited by barbarous nations.

---

[2] Charles-Pierre Claret, Comte de Fleurieu (1738–1810), navigator and statesman, born at Lyon, was the inventor of a chronometer and Minister of the Navy in 1790.

Assisting him was Captain de Langle, an officer of great ability who had proved himself in the operations against the English at Hudson Bay. Two transports armed as frigates, the *Boussole* and the *Astrolabe*, were fitted out at Brest for this new voyage around the world. La Pérouse himself commanded the *Boussole*, and the *Astrolabe* was under the orders of de Langle. The staff officers were chosen by the commander himself, and all of the officers honored by assignment to the expedition were distinguished by their intellectual superiority. Finally, scientists of every kind, who were to engage in research to advance the progress of human knowledge, completed the roster of this important project.[3]

The French vessels, supplied with excellent instruments, in particular chronometers for determining longitude, set sail from Brest roads, August 1, 1785. Thus began the chain of events related in this book. By a chronological leap, let us state that after two and a half years La Pérouse sailed into sight of Botany Bay, Australia, on January 21, 1788. His last letters were sent from this port. After that, the world retained no trace of him, nor did anyone receive any more news of him. Only some hazy statements occasionally recalled his name. The National Assembly, sensible of his misfortunes as well as of his glory, called upon all navigators, in the name of humanity and the arts and sciences, to send any information which could shed some light on the fate of the French expedition. Then, in 1791, it ordered two frigates to be fitted out as a search party. General D'Entrecasteaux,[4] who was placed in command of the expedition, carried out his instructions with painstaking care. He visited successively the Friendly Islands [Tonga Islands], New Caledonia, New Hebrides, and unwittingly passed by the island which concealed the survivors of the crews

---

[3] This brilliant company included the engineer Monneron, the astronomer Lepaute [Jean André Lepaute (1720–1789), clockmaker, born at Thonne-la-Long, Ardennes], the naturalists Lamanon, Monges [Abbé Monges, regular canon of the Catholic Church, served as chaplain on the *Boussole*], Lamartinière, and the famous Monge [Gaspard Monge, Comte de Peluse (1746–1818), mathematician, born at Beaune, inventor of descriptive geometry and one of the founders of the École Polytechnique] whose poor health forced him to land at Tenerife and to return to Europe.—Valentin

[4] Joseph-Antoine Bruni d'Entrecasteaux (1737–1793) became commander of the French fleet in the East Indies in 1785; in that capacity he made a voyage to China. His next, and last, assignment was the search for La Pérouse.

of the *Boussole* and the *Astrolabe*. He returned home without a scrap of information and without the slightest clue to the fate of La Pérouse.[5]

In another decree, the National Assembly ordered that the reports and charts sent back by La Pérouse, covering his travels as far as Botany Bay, be printed and engraved at public expense. The editorial work was entrusted to General Millet-Mureau, Corps of Engineers; the proceeds of the sale were given to the Rear Admiral's widow, whose grief it was to die without the consolation of knowing the fate of him whose destiny had been joined to hers.[6]

---

[5] An Englishman, Captain Dillon, first discovered evidence of the fate of La Pérouse and his intrepid company. Dillon's findings were later confirmed by Captain Dumont-d'Urville (1790–1842). The appendix contains the vivid details taken from d'Urville's own statement.—Valentin

[6] *The Voyage of La Pérouse* appeared in 1797, in three volumes in quarto, with an atlas and a portrait engraved by Tardieu.—Valentin

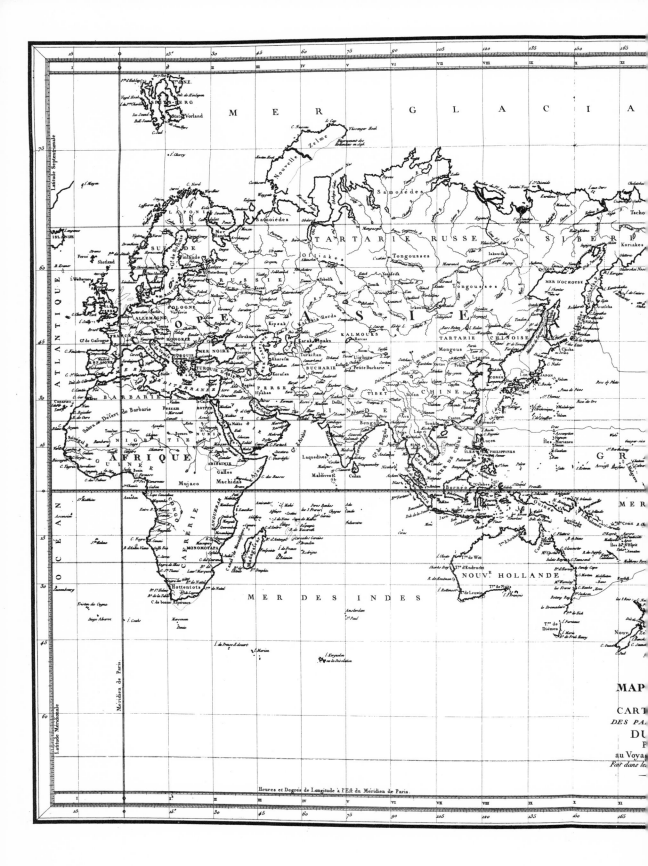

MER   GLACIA

MER   G L A C I A L E

I. Mayen

Latitude Septentrionale

ISLANDE

Shetland

MER D'OCHOTSK

RUSSIE

ATLANTIQUE

EUROPE   A S I E

TARTARIE RUSSE   ou   SIBER

Samoïedes

Samoïedes

LAPONIE

SUEDE DE

TARTARIE

Tongousses

Tongousses

MER NOIRE

TURQUIE D'

KALMOUKS

Mongous

TARTARIE CHINOISE

TURQUIE

BUCHARIE

Uïghurs   Petite Bucharie

JAPON

CHINE

MEDITERRANÉE

PERSE

TIBET

Delhi

INDE

COREE

Pekin

Canton

BARBARIE

Sahara ou Désert de Barbarie

NIGRITIE

NUBIE

Bengale   Ava

Golfe de Bengale

ILES DE LA CHINE

ILES   PHILIPPINES

G R

O C E A N

AFRIQUE
GUINEE

ABISSINIE
Galles
Machidas

Laquedives

Maldives   Ceilan

Borneo

Celebes

NOUV   Guinee

MER

CAFRERIE
ANGOUBER

Madagascar

NOUVᵉ HOLLANDE

Hottentots
C. de bonne Esperance

MER DES INDES

Amsterdam
I.ᵗ Paul

Tᵉ de
Diemen

Nouv.

Méridien de Paris

Latitude Méridionale

I. de Prince-Edouard
I. Marion

I. Kerguelen
ou la Desolation

MAP

CART

DES PA

DU

P

au Voya

Fait dans le

Heures et Degrés de Longitude à l'Est du Méridien de Paris.

Map of voyages

Voyages and Adventures of La Pérouse

CHAPTER I

The Crossing from Brest
 to Saint Catherine Island on the Brazilian Coast
Stop at Concepcion, Chile

THE CROSSING was uneventful until the expedition reached Madeira where the English trader, Johnston, gave the navigators a cordial reception. On August 9 they anchored at Tenerife. They immediately began work constructing an observatory ashore; the instruments were set up and the accuracy of the chronometers was tested by the elevations of the sun and the stars, in order to make the earliest possible corrections in the movements of the chronometers on the two frigates. As long as the French were in the roadstead, the governor-general of the Canary Islands treated them in the friendliest manner.

La Pérouse left Tenerife on August 30. The trip to the equator was made in the calmest weather. The northeast trade winds stopped at 14° north latitude, and the winds were steady from west to southwest. They forced the commander to follow the African coast for a distance of about sixty leagues.

On September 29, the expedition crossed the equator at 18° west longitude. There were no signs of land except for some frigate birds. In these latitudes, the ships were surrounded for a long time by tuna fish, but only a small number of them could be caught. These fish were so large that they broke all the lines. Each of those caught weighed at least sixty pounds.

On October 16, at ten o'clock in the morning, they sighted the Martin

Vas Islands. After determining their position, they sailed on a starboard tack toward the island of Trinidad [off the coast of Brazil], about nine leagues west-southwest of Martin Vas. Properly speaking, the Martin Vas Islands are only rocks; the largest may be a quarter league around. There are three islets, separated from each other by very short distances. When seen from afar, they look like five heads.

At sunset they saw the island of Trinidad, on a bearing of west 8° north. The wind was steady at north-northwest. They passed the whole night tacking about, remaining east-southeast of the island. At dawn, they continued the tack toward land, hoping to find calm water in the lee of the island. At ten o'clock in the morning, the southeast point of the island was about two and a half leagues north-northwest of them. Within the cove formed by this point, La Pérouse sighted a Portuguese flag raised above a small fort around which were grouped five or six wooden houses. The flag aroused his curiosity. He decided to send a boat ashore for information regarding the evacuation and cession of the island by the English.

Early the next day, October 18, when the *Astrolabe* was about a half league from land, she let loose her pinnace, commanded by Lieutenant Vaujuas. Two naturalists, Lamartinière and Father Receveur,[1] accompanied the lieutenant. They entered the center of the cove between two rocks; however, the waves were so high that the boat and her crew would certainly have been lost but for the prompt succour which the Portuguese gave them. They drew the boat ashore and placed it beyond the raging sea. Lieutenant Boutin, accompanied by the geologist Lamanon and the engineer Monneron, was also sent out with a boat but with orders not to go ashore if the *Astrolabe*'s pinnace arrived there first. Consequently, he only approached within musket range of the shore. He sounded the roadstead, and the soundings consistently indicated a bottom of rock mixed with a little sand. Monneron sketched the fort quite as well as if he had been on the beach, and Lamanon determined the rocks to be basalt or the lava of some extinct volcanoes. The island appears to be no more than an almost barren rock; some vegetation and a few bushes are visible in the narrow gorges of the mountains. On the southeast side of the island, the

---

[1] Father Receveur served as chaplain aboard the *Astrolabe*.

Portuguese had established their base in a valley about six hundred yards wide. No doubt the reason they occupied an island which can support neither men nor beasts was to prevent any other European nation from using it as a base for smuggling into Brazil.

When the two lieutenants reported that at Trinidad it was impossible to obtain the water and wood which the ships needed, La Pérouse immediately decided to proceed to Saint Catherine Island on the Brazilian coast, a customary stopping place for French ships en route to the Pacific Ocean. From noon of October 18, until evening of October 24, they proceeded west toward Ascension Island.[2] When he realized that he was wasting his time, La Pérouse gave up his search for this island.[3] On the 25th, they went through an extremely violent storm. From that day until their arrival at Saint Catherine, the weather was continually bad. The ships were enveloped in a fog thicker than any observed on the coasts of Brittany in the middle of winter. On November 6, they dropped anchor between Saint Catherine Island and the mainland, in seven fathoms, a silty bottom.

After ninety-six days at sea, there was not a single case of illness on board. The changing climate, the winds, the fogs, nothing had affected the health of the crews. As a matter of fact, the commander had carefully taken every precaution prescribed by prudence and experience to keep the supplies in good condition. Furthermore, he had sought to maintain morale by allowing the crews two hours of recreation every evening, weather permitting.

Saint Catherine Island extends from north to south a distance of about a dozen leagues. From east to west it is only two leagues wide. At the narrowest part, the channel separating it from the mainland is about four hundred yards wide. Overlooking this passage is the town of Nostra Senhora do Desterro, the island's capital. The land is very fertile and scarcely requires any cultivation to produce every kind of fruit, vegetable, and grain. It is covered with trees which are always green but are so interwoven with briers and twines that it is impossible to cross through

---

[2] Not to be confused with the island of the same name located northwest of St. Helena.—Valentin

[3] La Pérouse later came to the conclusion that this island was non-existent.

the forest except by carving a passage with a hatchet. Furthermore, these forests conceal a great number of reptiles whose bite is usually fatal. All the dwellings on the island are on the seashore. The woods which surround them diffuse afar a delightful fragrance, filled as they are with orange trees and aromatic trees and shrubs. Despite so many assets, the country is very poor. There is no manufacturing whatsoever, and the inhabitants are dressed in rags. Whaling is very profitable in these latitudes.

The arrival of the French ships alarmed the area. The various forts fired signal guns, whereupon La Pérouse dropped anchor promptly and sent a boat ashore with an officer, in order to declare his peaceful intentions and his need for water, wood, and fresh provisions. The officer charged with this business found the citadel's little garrison under arms. A bronze medal which La Pérouse sent to the governor convinced the latter of the object of the French visit. Orders were immediately issued to sell them whatever they needed at the most reasonable price possible. When he arrived at Saint Catherine, La Pérouse expected to resume his voyage after five or six days at the most, but the currents and the south winds were so violent that communication with the shore was frequently interrupted and the frigates' departure was delayed. Furthermore, members of the crews had nothing but praise for the hospitality of the island's inhabitants, as confirmed by the following incident. When the boat which La Pérouse had sent into a cove for wood was capsized by a billow, the islanders who helped to save it forced the stranded sailors to use their beds while they slept next to them on mats on the ground. A few days later, the islanders returned the sails, masts, grapnel, and flag of this pinnace, although these articles would have been most useful on their canoes.

On the evening of November 16, after taking on more than a month's supply of cattle, pigs, and poultry, the commander sent his mail to the governor, who agreed to forward it to the address of the French consul in Lisbon. Expecting to sail the next day, everyone wrote to his family and friends, but north winds kept the ships in the bay until the 19th. They weighed anchor at dawn, but a calm forced them to anchor again for a few hours and they did not get out to sea until nightfall.

The weather was perfect until the 28th when they experienced a very violent squall from the east, the first since leaving Brest. La Pérouse noted with satisfaction that, if his ships were slow, they stood up very well in bad weather and could easily make their way through the rough seas which they were going to encounter.

On December 7, their position was 44° 38' south latitude and 34° west longitude. They saw quantities of seaweed, and for several days the frigates were surrounded by petrels and albatrosses, which never approach land except during the breeding season. These slight indications of land strengthened the crews' hopes and gave them some consolation in their struggle against the horrendous sea. La Pérouse, however, was worried by the thought that he still had 35° westward to go to the Strait of Le Maire, which he had to reach before the end of January.

They tacked about in 44° and 45° south latitude until December 24. On the 25th, the winds were steady from the southwest and lasted several days. The winds forced La Pérouse to follow a west-northwest course and to leave the parallel which he had followed continuously for twenty days, having tried to ascertain the existence of Grande Island of La Roche. Since it was very late in the season, he decided to take the course which would bring him farthest westward; he feared the risk of doubling Cape Horn during the bad season. The weather, however, was more favorable than he had anticipated. The squalls stopped in December, and the month of January was at least as pleasant as July in Europe.

There were several days when the sea was calm and beautiful. The officers of the two frigates took advantage of these days to go out hunting in the ships' boats.

On these trips they killed a great number of birds, which were continually hovering around the ships. These consisted of four varieties of petrels and the larger and the smaller species of albatross. These birds, cooked with a piquant sauce, had a fairly good taste. The sailors preferred them to salt meat.

On January 14, 1786, they finally sounded bottom off the coast of Patagonia, at 47° 50' south latitude and 64° 37' west longitude. On the 21st they sighted Cape Buen Tiempo or the north point of Rio Gallegos, on the Patagonian coast, and at two o'clock on the 25th, at one league to the south, they raised Cape San Diego, which forms the western point of the Strait of Le Maire. At three o'clock they were in the strait. The wind was so favorable and the season so advanced that La Pérouse decided to lose no time in doubling Cape Horn. He plotted a course toward the Juan Fernandez Islands, which were on his way and where he could find water and wood as well as some fresh provisions superior to the penguins of the strait.

While the frigates were passing through the Strait of Le Maire, the savages, following their usual practice, lit great fires to induce the French to drop anchor. A half league from Tierra del Fuego they were surrounded by whales. It was soon evident that the creatures had never been bothered. The ships did not frighten them at all as they swam pompously within pistol range. The eastern horizon was so overcast that Staten Island [I. de los Estados] was not visible, even though it was only five leagues distant. They hugged the coast of Tierra del Fuego closely enough to see some savages through the spyglasses. These individuals were building great fires, which was their only way of expressing their desire to see the ships drop anchor.

The expedition doubled Cape Horn with much more ease than its commander had expected. On February 7, they were opposite the Strait of Magellan in the Pacific Ocean, on a course for the Juan Fernandez Islands. However, when La Pérouse noticed that his provisions were low and that the worms had begun to attack the ship's bread, he decided to sail for Concepcion, Chile, where he knew he could obtain ample supplies at a reasonable price.

In the evening of February 22, they raised Mocha Island, which is about fifty leagues south of Concepcion. The following day, at two o'clock, they doubled the point of Quinquirine Island [Quiriquina Island in Bay of Concepcion], but the winds, which had been from the south and had favored the expedition up to this time, became contrary. They sailed on different tacks, sounding continuously. La Pérouse searched in vain with his telescope for sight of the town of Concepcion, which, according to Frezier's map, he knew must be at the end of the bay on the southeast side, but he saw nothing. At five o'clock, pilots approached the ship and informed the commander that the town he was looking for had been destroyed by an earthquake in 1751, that it no longer existed, and that the new town had been built three leagues from the sea, on the banks of the Bobio River. They also informed him that he was expected in Concepcion and that letters from the Spanish minister had arrived there before him.

The crews continued to tack about in order to reach the end of the bay, and at nine o'clock they dropped anchor, in nine fathoms, about a league northwest of Talcahuano. At ten o'clock a Spanish naval captain, sent by the commanding officer of Concepcion, came on board. He ordered a large supply of fresh meat, fruit, and vegetables to be brought to the ships. The good health of the crews apparently surprised him; no vessel had ever doubled Cape Horn and arrived in Chile without some of the men becoming ill; but there was not one case of sickness on the two frigates.

At seven in the morning, February 24, they weighed anchor, and at eleven o'clock they moored in Talcahuano cove. The ruins of the old town of Concepcion were visible to the west. After the destruction of this town, its inhabitants were scattered and camped on the high ground nearby. It was not until 1763 that they selected a new site, a quarter league from the Bobio River and three leagues from the original Concepcion. There they built a new town to which the bishop's palace, the cathedral, and the religious houses were transferred. This city occupies an extensive area on the plain because the houses, which are built of clay or sun-baked bricks, have only one floor to make them less vulnerable to the earthquakes which occur almost every year. At that time the city had more than 10,000 inhabitants and was expected to increase in size and prosperity.

This part of Chile has a perfect climate. The return on wheat is at a ratio of sixty to one; grapes are equally productive. Countless cattle cover the countryside and, without any care, reproduce most prolifically. The inhabitants' only labor is to fence in their lands and to keep their cattle, horses, mules, and sheep inside the corrals. Unfortunately, the country produces gold; almost all the rivers are auriferous. The natives can earn half a dollar a day by washing the earth which conceals this troublesome metal. However, since the necessities of life are abundant, they have no other real needs prompting them to work. Knowing neither our skills nor our luxuries, they have not enough motivation to overcome their inertia. Even the houses of the richest people have no furniture. Nevertheless, they are extremely polite and obliging, as demonstrated by the reception given to La Pérouse and his companions.

The *Astrolabe* and the *Boussole* were hardly moored in front of the village of Talcahuano before the acting commandant came aboard and escorted La Pérouse and his officers to Concepcion. They stopped at the home of the artillery commander, whose name was Sabatero, where an excellent dinner was served them. In the evening, there was a great ball to which the town's leading ladies were invited. The Frenchmen were immensely impressed by the clothing of these ladies, which was quite different from what they were accustomed to. The costume consists of a pleated skirt extending from the hips to a few inches below the knee; red, white, and blue striped stockings; and shoes so short that they bend back all the toes so that the foot is almost round. Their hair is not powdered and is arranged in back in small braids reaching the shoulders. The blouse is usually made of gold or silver muslin. Over it are worn two mantillas. The first is of muslin; the second, worn over the first, is of varicolored wool. The woolen mantillas cover the ladies' heads when they go out of doors or in cold weather, but indoors they usually hold the mantillas on their knees. In general, the inhabitants of Concepcion are so hospitable that there is not a port in Europe which can equal them in this respect.

Before the French left Concepcion, Governor O'Higgins[4] returned from the frontier, where he had gone to negotiate with the Indians. Born in Ireland of one of the families persecuted for its religion and its traditional loyalty to the house of Stuart, O'Higgins had just rendered an important service to his adopted country by signing a peace treaty with the savages, who had continually been destroying isolated homesteads, slaughtering the men, old people, and children, and taking the women captive. In his courtesy to the members of the expedition, he outdid the acting governor.

Before his departure, La Pérouse decided to provide a great celebration and to invite all the ladies of Concepcion. For this purpose they raised a pavilion on the beach. More than one hundred and fifty men and women did not mind traveling three leagues to accept the invitation of the Frenchmen. They enjoyed a great feast, which was followed by a ball. The festivities ended with a display of fireworks and the spectacular ascent of a large paper balloon.

---

[4] Ambrosio O'Higgins was governor of Chile from 1778 to 1795 and viceroy of Peru from 1795 to 1801. His natural son was Bernardo O'Higgins (1776–1842), the champion of Chilean independence and head of the first permanent national government of Chile.

CHAPTER II

Arrival at Easter Island
Description of the Island—The Native Customs
Stop at the Hawaiian Islands

LA PÉROUSE never permitted pleasure to interfere with the serious business of his voyage. On March 15, after he had repaired his ships and taken on the necessary water and wood, he gave the order to weigh anchor, but the south wind did not allow his departure until the 19th. He steered a course for the Juan Fernandez Islands but never sighted them. On the 23rd, the ships' position was 30° 29′ south latitude and 85° 52′ west longitude. On the 24th, the winds became steady from the east and did not vary by as much as 5° until the expedition was about one hundred twenty leagues from Easter Island. They raised this island April 8, and the next day the two ships dropped anchor in Cook Bay. A great number of natives, brimming over with good spirits, visited the ships. La Pérouse, warned by the reports of different navigators, knew that these men were like big children, unable to resist the sight of European articles, and would resort to every trick to acquire them. Believing he could restrain them by fear, he ordered an armed party ashore. This landing was made with four boats and twelve marines. All the officers, except those needed to manage the two ships, accompanied the commander. The escort, consisting of the ships' crews, numbered seventy men.

Four or five hundred islanders were on the shore awaiting the Frenchmen. Unarmed, some were covered with white or yellow clothing, but the great majority were naked. Several were tattooed and had their faces painted red. Their shouts and expressions indicated happiness. They moved forward to greet the strangers and to assist their landing.

This part of the island has an elevation of about twenty feet; the mountains are about a mile inland. The land slopes gently from the foot of the mountains to the sea. This area is covered with a plant which La Pérouse believed suitable for grazing cattle. The plant conceals large stones which lie about on the ground. To the commander it looked like the same plant which grows in the Ile-de-France [Mauritius] where it is called *giraumons*[1] and produces the same size fruit. The stones are a natural asset, although they made walking inconvenient for the French. They keep the earth cool and moist, to some extent making up for the valuable shade trees which the natives foolishly cut down ages ago. As a result, the soil had been hardened by exposure to the burning rays of the sun, leaving the islanders without springs, brooks, or other water courses.

After landing, the commander's first task was to establish a perimeter by deploying his troops in a circle. The inhabitants were ordered to keep out of this area. After pitching a tent, the party brought ashore the livestock and the goods which were to be given to the natives. However, since La Pérouse had explicitly forbidden the troops to fire, and since his orders even forbade them to use their musket butts on those who pressed too close, the soldiers were soon subjected to the rapaciousness of a growing number of natives. There were at least eight hundred, including more than one hundred fifty women, several of whom were quite attractive. While some of them distracted the foreigners, others removed the foreigners' hats and kerchiefs. All appeared to be accomplices to the thefts which were being committed, for scarcely were these deeds done when, like a flight of birds, they all fled at the same instant. When they saw that the French did not make any use of their muskets, they returned in a few minutes and watched for the moment to perpetrate another act of larceny. This game lasted the whole morning. Since the ships were to leave that night, there was too little time for the officers to attempt to educate these savages, so the French relaxed by watching the tricks used in stealing. Finally, to remove any excuse for coming to blows, since this could have

---

[1] A cucurbitaceous plant such as the pumpkin.

had the most tragic consequences, La Pérouse announced that he would replace the hats stolen from the soldiers and sailors. The natives were unarmed; only three or four had a kind of wooden club which did not appear dangerous. Some seemed to have authority over the others. La Pérouse took these persons to be chiefs, but he did not wait to see if they were, likewise, the most outstanding thieves.

"We had," wrote La Pérouse, "only eight or ten hours for our stay on the island, and we did not want to lose any time. Accordingly, I ordered M. d'Escures, my first lieutenant, to place a guard on the tent and all of our property, and I put him in command of all soldiers and sailors ashore. We then divided ourselves into two sections. The first, under M. de Langle, was to advance as far as possible into the interior of the island, to plant seeds wherever they seemed likely to grow, and to examine the soil, the vegetation, the culture, the people, the statues, and generally everything of interest on this remarkable island. Those who felt strong enough for a long march went with M. de Langle. The other section, of which I was a member, merely visited the statues, the platforms, the homes and gardens within a league of our base. The drawings of these statues, made by Hodges,[2] artist of the Cook expedition, are quite inaccurate when compared with the actual objects. Forster[3] believed that they were the work of a very much larger population than the present one, but I consider his opinion unfounded. The largest of the great statues which are on these platforms and which we measured is only 14 feet 6 inches high, 6 feet 6 inches wide at the shoulders, 3 feet thick at the waist, 6 feet wide and 5 feet thick at the base. These busts, I believe, are the work of the present population which, without any exaggeration, I estimate to be about two thousand persons. There are almost as many women as men, and I have seen as many children as in any other country. Since there were not more than three hundred women in the crowd of twelve hundred attracted to the bay by our arrival, I concluded that the natives on the other side of the

---

[2] William Hodges was the artist with Cook's second expedition (1772–1775).
[3] John Reinhold Forster and his son were engaged by the admiralty to accompany Cook on his second voyage and to explore and collect the natural history of the places they visited.

Natives and monuments of Easter Island

island had come to see our ships and that the women, either indisposed or busy with their children and households, had stayed at home, so that we saw only the women who lived in the vicinity of the bay. M. de Langle's report confirmed this opinion; on the other side of the island he met many women and children.

"All of us went into the caves where Forster and some of Captain Cook's officers at first believed the women could have been hidden. These are underground dwellings. It is entirely possible that the natives might have hidden their women here when Captain Cook stopped at these islands in 1772,[4] but I am unable to guess why. We are perhaps indebted to Cook's benevolence toward these people for the confidence which they have shown us, which has placed us in a better position to estimate their population.

"All of the statues which we saw and which our artist, M. Duché [Duché de Vancy], sketched very accurately, appeared to be quite old. The dead are placed in *marae* or tombs, as far as can be judged from the great number of bones found. The form of government here has now declined to such an extent that they no longer have a chief of sufficient importance to merit the great amount of labor required for preserving his memory through the erection of a statue.

"The most noteworthy of the pyramids which we saw was coated with whitewash. These cairns, which represent an hour's work for one man, are piled up along the sea coast. By lying upon the ground, an Indian showed us that these stones cover a grave. Then, by raising his hands to heaven, he unquestionably wanted us to understand that the natives believe in a life hereafter. I was at first very skeptical about this interpretation, since I considered these people too primitive for such a concept, but after seeing the sign repeated several times and after M. de Langle, who had traveled into the island's interior, reported the same observation to me, I no longer had any doubt regarding this. However, we discovered no trace of any religious cult, since I do not believe that anyone could take the statues for idols, even though the Indians treat them with great veneration. These

---

[4] Cook began his second voyage in 1772, but he arrived at Easter Island about a year later.

gigantic busts, which show how little progress the natives have achieved in sculpture, are made of a volcanic product known to scientists as *lapillo* [tuff]. This stone is so soft and light that some of Captain Cook's officers believed it was artificial, made of a kind of mortar which hardened on exposure to the air. We still have to explain how they managed to raise so great a weight without a fulcrum. The volcanic rock is very light, and with levers thirty or thirty-five feet long, by sliding stones underneath, it is possible to raise a much greater weight. One hundred men are enough for this task. There is nothing marvelous about this explanation which has the added advantage of restoring to nature the *lapillo*, a stone which is definitely not artificial, as was formerly believed."

Scarcely a tenth of the island is cultivated; nevertheless, La Pérouse thought that in three days of working each native could provide himself with enough food for a year. Each village or district has its communal houses. Measured by the French captain, one of these houses is three hundred ten feet long, ten feet wide, and ten feet high at the center. It is shaped like an overturned canoe. The only entrances are two doors, each two feet high, so that one enters by crawling in on his hands and knees. This house can accommodate more than two hundred persons. Together with two or three small dwellings a short distance away, this building forms an entire village. There are some underground homes; the others are constructed of reeds arranged in artistic designs, and they provide perfect protection from the rain. The structure is supported by a pillar of hewn stone, eighteen inches thick. Holes bored at regular intervals support poles which are crossed to form a vault-like framework. Reed mats cover the spaces between the poles.

At one o'clock in the afternoon, La Pérouse returned to the tent, intending to go back on board so that Captain Clonard,[5] his second in command, could have his turn ashore. There he found almost everyone minus his hat and kerchief. The crew's tolerance boldened the thieves, who spared none, not even the commander. One savage, after helping him down from a platform, removed the commander's hat and then fled as fast as his legs

---

[5] Sutton de Clonard, second in command of the *Boussole*, was put in full command of the *Astrolabe* after de Langle's massacre.

could carry him, followed, as usual, by all the others. La Pérouse did not order a pursuit, being unwilling to enjoy the exclusive privilege of shade while all his companions were bare-headed.

A short time later, two of the *Astrolabe*'s officers came with information that the savages had committed another theft, which led to a brawl between the savages and some sailors. Divers had cut the ship's cable and made off with the grapple. The theft was not discovered until the guilty ones had reached the interior of the island. Since the grapple was a very useful article, two officers and several soldiers pursued the thieves. Overwhelmed by a hail of stones, the soldiers fired a blank charge; but this had no effect, so they were forced to fire a round of small shot, some of which struck one of the savages. The musket fire frightened the thieves, and the officers had no difficulty in returning to the tent; but the grapple was not recovered. A little while later, the savages reappeared in the vicinity of the French base, and friendly relations were renewed as if nothing had disturbed them. To cap this description of the natives, at the very moment when Captain de Langle was presenting a pair of goats to one of the chiefs, this fellow accepted them with one hand and stole Captain de Langle's kerchief with the other. These people certainly do not have the same opinion of theft as we; they evidently do not consider it at all immoral. Yet they are not unaware that by stealing they are committing an injustice, since they flee as soon as they have taken something, obviously in order to avoid punishment.

La Pérouse observed the same culture on Easter Island as in the Society Islands but at a much lower level of achievement due to the lack of raw materials. The Easter Island canoes have the same design but are made of very narrow planks, four or five feet long, and can carry no more than four men. Furthermore, the natives make very little use of them; they are such expert swimmers that even in the heaviest seas they go two leagues from shore, and when they return they enjoy finding the spot where the waves break with the greatest force.

Fishing is poor in the coastal waters, and the islanders depend entirely upon plant life for their subsistence. They eat yams, arrowroot, bananas, sugar cane, and a small fruit which grows on the rocky shores and resembles the grapes found on the tropical coasts of the Atlantic.

They cultivate their fields with great skill. They grub up the weeds, heap them and burn them, and fertilize the soil with the ashes. Their banana trees are planted in straight rows. They also grow a species of nightshade (*solanum*). Their culinary technique is the same as that used in the Society Islands. A hole is hollowed out in the ground, their yams or tubers are covered with hot stones or with a mixture of embers and earth, and in this way all their food is oven-baked.

The care which they took in measuring the French ships demonstrated to La Pérouse that they were intelligent enough to appreciate our technical accomplishments. They closely examined our cables, the anchors, the compass, the steering wheel, and returned the next day to repeat their inspection. This led the captain to believe that there had been discussion ashore which left them with some doubts concerning our equipment. This investigation definitely proved that they were capable of reflection, as already shown by their conduct in the presence of firearms, since merely aiming a musket made them flee. This discovery, however, actually made a disagreeable impression upon the minds of their visitors, who left with a very low estimate of the islanders and much dissatisfaction with the way they had accepted the help which the French wanted to give them.

After leaving some European domestic animals and planting some seeds in this land of thieves, La Pérouse quit Cook's Bay on April 10, 1786, but he was not out of sight of it until the next day. The winds held steady from southeast to east-southeast until the 17th. The weather was perfectly clear; it did not change until it became overcast when the winds shifted to east-northeast, where they remained from the 17th until the 20th. The men then began to catch tuna, which followed the frigates all the way to the Sandwich Islands [Hawaiian Islands] and provided a complete ration for the crews almost every day for a month and a half. This excellent nourishment kept them in the best of health. They were now sailing in unknown seas, following a route parallel to that taken by Captain Cook in 1777 when he sailed from the Society Islands to the northwest coast of America. Since La Pérouse hoped to discover something in a track of almost two thousand leagues, sailors were continuously up on the masts, and a prize was promised to the first man who sighted land. In order to observe a larger area, the frigates sailed abreast during the day, keeping an interval of three or four leagues.

On May 2, in 8° north latitude, they noticed many petrels as well as some frigate and tropic birds. Many turtles also passed the ships; the two which were caught were very good eating. From the appearance of these creatures, La Pérouse concluded that he had passed nearby some island which probably was uninhabited, since a rocky spot in the middle of the ocean would suit them better than a populated country. On the 15th, they were in 19° 17' north latitude and 130° west longitude, that is, in the same latitude as a group of islands placed on Spanish maps as well as that of the Hawaiian Islands. La Pérouse thought that by continuing his course to the latter group he would perform a valuable service to geographers if he succeeded in determining the exact position of the islands which the English had not been able to explore, especially Maui, and to clear the charts of useless names of islands which do not exist but only perpetuate errors dangerous to navigators. On the morning of May 28, he sighted the snow-capped mountains of Hawaii and, soon afterwards, the peaks of Maui, not quite so high as those of the first island. He pressed sail to reach land but was still seven or eight leagues away at nightfall. He spent the night tacking, awaiting daybreak to enter the channel between these two islands and to find an anchorage to the leeward of Maui. At nine o'clock in the morning, they raised the point of this island to the west. Enchanted by its beauty, they sailed one league along the coast, which led them to the channel on a bearing of southwest one-quarter west. Water cascades from the mountain tops, irrigating the native villages before it enters the sea. The dwellings are so numerous that a single village extends for three or four leagues. All the houses are at the edge of the sea, and the mountains are so near that the habitable land does not appear to be more than a quarter-league wide. Imagine the feelings of the poor sailors, who, in this hot climate, had been reduced to a water ration of one bottle a day, when they saw the mountains clothed in vegetation, the homes surrounded by green banana trees! But the sea broke upon the shore with the greatest force so that, like a modern Tantalus, the men could do no more than feast their eyes upon the treasures which they were unable to touch.

There was a strong breeze speeding them on at two leagues an hour.

La Pérouse wanted to complete his observation of this part of the island as far as Molokini before nightfall, hoping to find an anchorage sheltered from the trade winds hard by Molokini. This plan, demanded by the exigencies of the situation, did not allow him to shorten sail in order to wait for about one hundred fifty canoes which were launched from the shore and were bringing fruits and pigs to be exchanged with the strangers for pieces of iron.

Almost all of these canoes reached the frigates, but La Pérouse continued his course with so much speed that the ships' wake swamped them and capsized them. The islanders had to cast off the line which had been thrown to them, and they took to the water. They raised their canoes on their shoulders, emptied them, and cheerfully climbed back in, trying by dint of paddling to catch up with the frigates. Meanwhile, others who came out to the ships went through the same experience. In this way more than fifty canoes were overturned, so it was impossible for the French to obtain more than fifteen pigs and some fruit from the natives, even though the exchange was of great mutual advantage.

The canoes are equipped with outriggers and each carries from three to five men. On the average, the craft are about twenty-four feet long, one foot in beam, and nearly the same in depth. They do not weigh more than fifty pounds. Frail as these boats are, the islanders nevertheless can travel up to sixty leagues in them, crossing channels twenty leagues wide. The natives are such good swimmers that they stand comparison with seals and sea lions.

As the ships moved ahead, the mountains seemed to recede into the interior of the island, which gradually assumed the form of a titanic, greenish-yellow amphitheater. There were no more waterfalls to be seen, and the villages consisted of only ten or twelve widely separated huts— a great contrast to the country which was being left behind! The French did not find a sheltered area until they reached a shore made hideous by an ancient lava flow.

The ships anchored about a third of a league from land. They were sheltered from inshore winds by a large hill capped by clouds which from time to time produced violent squalls. Another disadvantage of this road-stead was the presence of currents which made it difficult to keep the

French frigates moored at Maui

ships headed into the wind. The natives of this part of the island were eager to come out in their canoes and trade with the strangers. For this purpose, they brought bananas and taro roots, as well as cloth and other unusual objects which they were wearing. La Pérouse did not allow them to climb aboard until the frigates were moored and the sails furled; he told them that it was *tabu,* a word which in their language signifies an object that their religion forbids them to touch. This statement had all the effectiveness which he anticipated it would. Captain de Langle, who did not take the same precaution, suddenly saw his frigate's deck clogged with a crowd of these savages, but they were so easy to manage that they were soon directed back into their canoes.

At eight o'clock in the morning of the following day, the French went ashore in four boats. The first two carried twenty armed soldiers. La Pérouse and all the officers and civilians whose duties did not require them to remain on board were in the other two. This party, which was prepared to prevent the sort of tragic misfortune which recently befell Captain Cook, did not frighten the natives. More than one hundred and twenty of them, men, women, and children, had been out in their canoes since the crack of dawn and immediately offered to begin trading. Two of them, who seemed to be men of authority, approached. They made a long, serious speech to La Pérouse, who did not understand a single word, and presented him with a pig, which he accepted. In return he gave them some medals, hatchets, and pieces of iron, which they valued very highly. By this generosity, the French succeeded in winning the friendship of the islanders.

During his reconnaissance, La Pérouse saw four small villages of ten or twelve houses. These are made of grass and are covered with the same material. They have the same shape as the thatched cottages found in certain parts of France. The roofs are pitched on two sides, and the door, which is located on the gable end, is only three feet high, so that it is necessary to stoop when entering. The furnishings consist of mats, which like our carpets make a very neat flooring on which the islanders sleep. The only cooking utensils they have are gourds painted in various colors. Their cloth is made from the paper mulberry tree, but, although painted in a great variety of colors, it appears less skillfully made than the cloth of other South Sea islanders.

When he returned aboard, the commander learned that Captain Clonard, his executive officer, had received a chief and had bought a cape and a fine red helmet from him; he had also acquired more than one hundred pigs, some bananas, yams, taro, mats, and various small objects made of feathers and shells. The frigates, however, were dragging their anchors; there was a very strong breeze from the east-southeast. It was necessary to give the signal to get under way, but they could not weigh anchor until five o'clock in the afternoon. Until eight o'clock, the breeze was continually shifting so that they were unable to make even half a league. The wind finally held steady at north-northwest. La Pérouse followed a course to the west, passing midway between the northwest point of the island of Kahoolawe and the southwest point of Lanai. At daybreak, he steered for the southwest point of the island of Molokai and followed its coast at a distance of three-quarters of a league, leaving it to enter the channel which separates the island of Oahu from Molokai. On June 1 at six o'clock in the evening, all the islands were behind them. La Pérouse had reconnoitered the archipelago in less than forty-eight hours and had accomplished his objective of clarifying an important geographical point by removing five or six non-existent islands from the maps of the Spanish cartographers.

CHAPTER III

Departure from the Hawaiian Islands
Northwest Coast of North America
Frenchmen's Harbor—The Expedition's First Disaster
Description of Frenchmen's Harbor
Manners and Customs of the Inhabitants

THE FRIGATES' COURSE was toward the northwest coast of America. As soon as they had left the anchorage at Maui, they no longer saw the great schools of fish which had followed them for a distance of almost fifteen hundred leagues from Easter Island. The cause of their disappearance was evidently the lower temperature of the water, which they could not tolerate. On June 9, in 34° north latitude, the weather became foggy and very humid. The mist or rain penetrated the sailors' clothing. To prevent scurvy, which is caused chiefly by dampness, La Pérouse ordered pails full of live coals to be placed in the forecastle and between-decks where the crew slept. Each man was issued a pair of boots, and the heavy woolen clothing which had been stowed away after leaving the waters of Cape Horn was returned to the men. As a tonic, quinine was mixed with the morning grog, in amounts small enough not to affect the flavor of the beverage.

These measures were not the only matters which concerned the French during so long a crossing. In order to insure an ample supply of flour and hardtack, a quantity of parched wheat, which was expected not to spoil, was taken on before leaving Brest. To grind it, the ships were equipped with mills which could be operated by four men. However, when the machines were tried, they broke the grain but did not grind it. Fortunately, Captain de Langle's inventiveness and the assistance of a sailor who had previously been a miller's apprentice overcame the setback. He rigged the little mills up in the same manner as windmills and at first had some success with sails turned by the wind, but he soon replaced them with a crank. In this way, they produced flour of quality as excellent as that of ordinary mills, each day grinding two hundredweight of wheat.

During the crossing from the Hawaiian Islands to the North American coast, the winds remained favorable. As they progressed, the mariners observed more and more of a species of seaweed entirely new to them. Shaped like a hose, it was forty to fifty feet long, ending in a spherical body the size of an orange. Huge whales, mergansers, and ducks also indicated that land was near. It appeared finally on June 23, at four o'clock in the morning. The fog suddenly disappeared and revealed a long range of snowcapped mountains. Bering's Mt. St. Elias was identified, with its peak visible above the clouds. The sight of land, which normally gladdens men after a long voyage, did not have the usual effect upon our mariners. The visual impact of these masses of snow covering a sterile, treeless soil was painful; the mountains appeared close to the sea, which breaks against a shelf of land more than a thousand feet high. There is a striking contrast between the great ledge, bare and blackened as if by fire, and the white snows seen beyond the clouds.

On the 25th during the entire day, a thick fog blotted out the land, but on the 26th the weather was perfect. The land appeared clearly at two o'clock in the morning, and the expedition sailed along the coast for two leagues. La Pérouse finally concluded that he had come upon a harbor. One of the officers, the Chevalier de Monti, was sent with three boats to make a reconnaissance. He reported that in this area the coast recedes a considerable distance toward the northwest but provides no shelter from the winds. The sea breaks heavily upon the shore, which is covered with driftwood. This bay was named Monti Bay.

La Pérouse next sighted the Bering River, and at noon on July 2, at 58° 36′ north latitude and 140° 31′ west longitude, he raised Mount Fairweather. At two o'clock, he discovered an indentation which seemed to be a fine bay. He steered his course toward it. Two officers from each frigate were sent to make a reconnaissance of the area. On the basis of the favorable report which they received, the frigates advanced toward the channel. The savages soon appeared and signaled their friendliness by waving white capes. Several of their canoes were fishing in the bay where the water is as calm as in an anchorage. This hitherto uncharted harbor is located thirty-three leagues from the port of Los Remedios, the extreme limit of Spanish navigation on this coast, about two hundred twenty-four leagues from Nootka and two hundred leagues from William's Sound. The calm within the bay quite delighted the seafarers, since it was absolutely necessary for them to refit and to change almost the entire stowage. La Pérouse named the place Frenchmen's Harbor [Lituya Bay]. At six o'clock in the morning, July 3, the ships passed the entrance and anchored a half-cable's length from shore, but not without the risk of being wrecked, pushed as they were by a west-northwest wind, which came up suddenly and carried them into the bay with frightful force.

As soon as the French had anchored in the bay, almost all the savages in the vicinity came to them in canoes loaded with a large amount of otter pelts, which they very eagerly traded for adzes, hatchets, and iron bars. At first they gave salmon for pieces of old barrel-hoops, but they soon became less obliging, and this fish could not be had except for nails or some small iron implements.

La Pérouse set up his observation post on an island located within the inlet not more than a musket shot from the ships. There the French established a base for rest and repairs. Tents were erected for the sail-makers and the blacksmiths, and a depot was set up for the water casks from the holds where the dunnage was being completely replaced.

On this island the French expected to be safe from the rapacity of the natives on the mainland; they soon learned differently. The savages spent every night watching for an opportunity to steal, but an effective guard was kept on board the ships. The natives became so aggressive that La Pérouse was forced to remove his base. At night they would land along the coast, move through woods too dense for the French to penetrate, and then, crawling on their bellies like adders without disturbing so much as a leaf, they managed to pilfer various articles, despite the watchfulness of the guards. The night they reached the height of cunning was when they entered the tent which lodged Dardau and Lauriston, the officers of the shore guard. Without being observed by any of the twelve men on duty, they removed a silver-mounted musket and the clothes of the two officers, who had taken the precaution of putting them under the heads of their cots.

These difficulties did not prevent the ships' pinnaces and longboats from getting water and wood. All the officers were continually on duty, in charge of work details which had to be sent ashore. Their presence in great numbers impressed the savages. During this period, the engineers, Monneron and Bernizet, made a survey of the bay in a well-armed pinnace. To have an accurate idea of this bay, imagine a basin so deep its center cannot be sounded, surrounded by very high mountains whose peaks are covered with snow, without a blade of grass on these huge, rocky heaps doomed by nature to eternal sterility. No breeze ever ripples the water's surface; only gigantic pieces of ice disturb it as they break off the various glaciers and fall with a crashing sound which echoes among the distant mountains. The air is so calm, the silence so profound that a man's voice can be heard more than half a league away, as well as can be heard the noise of the sea birds which come to lay their eggs in the rocky crevices.

At the end of this bay La Pérouse hoped to find channels by which he could penetrate the interior of North America. He believed that some great river, rising in one of the great Canadian lakes and flowing down between the two mountains, emptied into it. This belief, however, was only a dream. After proceeding by boat for about a league and a half, the commander and several of his officers saw the bay ending in two immense glaciers. To enter this inlet, they had to make their way through the floes which covered the water. Captain de Langle and several other officers wanted to clamber up the glacier. They exhausted themselves after they had gone two leagues and taken great risks crossing the deepest crevasses. Before them the snow and ice extended endlessly.

The principal objective, however, which had been the reason for anchoring in the bay, was accomplished. The boats were back in place and the holds re-stowed. Stores of wood and water were replenished and the engineers had completed their survey when a frightful accident, the first of a long series of misfortunes which finally ended in a double shipwreck, befell the hitherto successful expedition.

On July 13, three boats under the command of Lieutenant d'Escures left to make soundings in the bay. Since this officer's precipitancy had been noticed on several occasions, La Pérouse believed it necessary to give him written instructions, chief of which was not to approach the channel leading into the bay before the time the sea became slack, because the entrance was blocked by a dangerous bar where breakers formed when the tide was flowing. The boats left at six o'clock in the morning. At ten o'clock, La Pérouse was astonished to see Lieutenant Boutin bringing back the *Boussole*'s boat. This officer's appearance was far from reassuring; his face was stamped with anguish. Before long, he reported the frightful disaster which he had escaped only because his boldness and presence of mind immediately enabled him to use the resources available to him in a critical emergency. D'Escures, thinking he was still far from the channel, was suddenly seized by the current. Despite the superhuman efforts of his oarsmen to pull the boat to safety, the craft and all who were in it were instantly engulfed. Swept along as he followed his commander into the midst of the breakers which were rushing into the channel while the tide was going out at the speed of three or four leagues an hour, Lieutenant Boutin skillfully turned his boat's stern into the waves. In this way, by yielding to the waves which struck it, the boat avoided being swamped but was nevertheless swept out backwards by the tide. Presently he saw the breakers in front of his boat and found himself on the high sea. More concerned for his comrades' safety than for his own, he skirted the breakers in a rescue attempt, but all of his efforts were in vain. He was continuously forced back by the tide, and he went through the anguish of seeing his unfortunate fellow countrymen perish instantaneously while he was unable to bring them any help.

A few moments later, Captain de Langle arrived to tell La Pérouse that the disaster was even worse than he believed. The *Astrolabe*'s longboat shared the tragic fate of the *Boussole*'s boat. This craft, commanded by the two Laborde brothers,[1] was beyond the reach of the current when d'Escures was wrecked. These noble officers, taking counsel only of their courage, did not hesitate to come to the help of their companions and

---

[1] Laborde-Marchainville and Laborde-Boutervilliers.—Valentin

perished with them. De Langle, a kind and sympathetic person, wept profoundly while he described this sorrowful episode. Since his departure from France, he had made it a practice never to detail the two brothers to the same assignment, and it was only on this fatal occasion that he had yielded to the brothers, who were deeply attached to each other, when they requested to go out hunting together.

The savages also came out in their canoes to report the tragic occurrence; by their signs, these crude fellows indicated that they had seen the destruction of the two boats and that any rescue would have been impossible. The French heaped gifts upon them and tried to make them understand that all of the ships' bounty would be bestowed upon anyone who succeeded in saving a single man. Nothing was more likely to arouse their sympathies; they went along the shores and spread out on both sides of the bay. La Pérouse had already sent his longboat, under the command of Captain Clonard, toward the east, where in the unlikely case that there were any survivors they would have come to shore. Captain de Langle proceeded westward to the seacoast, to make certain that every area was examined. Almost all of the officers volunteered to join in these gloomy searches. They went three leagues along the seacoast without finding the slightest bit of wreckage. The commander, who had remained on board with enough of the crews to handle the two ships, had kept up his hopes, for human nature is almost incapable of making a sudden transition from a state of happiness to one of profound anguish. The return of the longboats, however, ended this illusion and cast everyone into a condition of inexpressible discouragement.

There was nothing left for the French to do now but to leave the country which had become the scene of their tragedy. Yet they owed it to the families of their unfortunate friends to remain a few more days in this land of desolation. Too rapid a departure would have occasioned doubts and fears in Europe. La Pérouse, therefore, decided to wait several days. It was impossible to recover the bodies of the twenty-one victims, and on July 30, eighteen days after the fatal occurrence, he finally decided to set sail. Before departing, he erected, on the island in the middle of the bay, a monument to the dead. He named it Cenotaph Island. The following inscription was buried in a bottle at the foot of the cenotaph:

Two boats founder at Frenchmen's Harbor

TWENTY-ONE BRAVE SAILORS
PERISHED AT THE ENTRANCE TO THIS HARBOR:
WHOSOEVER YOU MAY BE,
MINGLE YOUR TEARS WITH OURS.

During his forced stay at Frenchmen's Harbor, La Pérouse collected a great amount of information on the assets and liabilities of the area, on its mineral and plant products, and on the manners and customs of the savages. The bay is located at 58° 37′ north latitude and 139° 50′ west longitude. The climate of the coast is immeasurably milder than that of Hudson Bay. Plant growth is very rapid during three or four months of the year. Near the shore they found celery, round-leafed sorrel, wild peas, yarrow, chicory, and monkey flower. Daily, at every meal, the crew's copper was filled with these vegetables. The forests provide an ample supply of strawberries, raspberries, and currants; the rivers, trout and salmon. In the bay, however, the crew caught only halibut, some of which weighed over one hundred pounds, some small rockfish, and other fish known on the coasts of France.

In the forests the hunters saw bears, martens, and squirrels, and the natives traded pelts of black and brown bears, Canadian lynx, ermine, and red fox.

Although the plant and animal life of this region greatly resembles that of many other places, its appearance cannot be compared with that of any country, and the deep valleys of the Alps and the Pyrenees have a less appalling effect on the beholder. The primeval mountains of granite and slate, covered with perpetual snow, destitute of trees and verdure, rise from the ocean's edge where their base forms a great quay. They are so steep that even the wild goats cannot climb higher than about six hundred yards. The valleys which separate them are filled with immense glaciers, extending from the horizon to the sea.

So frightening a land must naturally have inhabitants as different from civilized people as the region just described differs from the cultivated countryside of Europe. As crude and barbarous as their earth is stony and untilled, these men live on the land only to despoil it; at war with all its animals, they scorn the plant life which grows around them. La Pérouse saw women and children eating strawberries and raspberries, but he thought that these fruits must be a tasteless dish to those to whom the earth means no more than it means to the vultures of the air or the wolves and tigers of the forest.

Living, as they do, without any form of political organization, they are continually excited by fear or by desire for vengeance; violent and irascible, they are ceaselessly armed against one another. Risking starvation in winter because of the inutility of hunting, during the summer they enjoy the greatest abundance, since in less than an hour, they can catch enough fish for their families. Idle the remainder of the day, they spend it gambling, for which they are as avid as certain residents of our great cities. This is the principal cause of their quarrels.

During the entire time the French stopped in the bay, the savages in their canoes were always around the frigates; they spent three or four hours there before they started their barter of a few fish, or two or three otter pelts. They seized every opportunity to steal. They removed any iron objects which they were able to lift, and they were especially alert for any means by which they could, during the night, overcome the vigilance of the guards. La Pérouse invited some of their important persons on board and loaded them with gifts; the very men whom he treated with the greatest regard and courtesy never hesitated to steal a nail or an old pair of breeches. When the savages tried to smile pleasantly, it was a sure sign that they had stolen something. At the commander's suggestion, all members of the crew treated the children affectionately and gave them little gifts; the parents, however, were absolutely indifferent to these friendly gestures. When they asked to come on board with their children, it was only to satisfy their thievish propensities, and more than one father took advantage of the attention given his son to snatch whatever was close at hand and hide it under his fur cloak.

The French went ashore only in armed parties. The savages were so afraid of the muskets that eight or ten armed men could control a whole village. By the term "village" is meant three or four wooden sheds, twenty-five feet long and fifteen to twenty feet wide, covered only on the windward side with planks or bark; in the center is a fire over which fish are hung to dry in the smoke. Eighteen to twenty persons live in each of

A native fishing camp at Frenchmen's Harbor

these sheds, the women and children on one side, the men on the other. Each lodge forms a little independent community, with its own canoe and its own headman; members of a lodge leave the village and go out of the bay, bringing back their fish and lumber without the rest of the village apparently paying them the slightest attention. The filth and stench of the sheds are worse than in the den of any known animal. The savages never take as much as two steps to attend to their natural needs; on these occasions they seek neither shade nor privacy. They never wash the wooden bowls in which they boil their fish; the food is cooked, served, and eaten from the same vessel. Since these bowls cannot be placed on the fire, the water is boiled by means of red-hot stones which they replace until the food is completely cooked. They also know how to broil food, applying the same technique used by our soldiers in the field. During the summer, they wander from one bay to another, searching for food like sea wolves; in the winter, they penetrate the interior of the country to hunt beaver and other animals whose pelts they frequently brought to the French. Although they always go barefoot, the soles of their feet are not at all calloused, and they are unable to walk on stones, which proves that they travel only by canoe or on snow with snowshoes.

Dogs are the only animals which they have befriended; there are usually three or four of them in each lodge. They are small and resemble Buffon's sheep dog. Instead of barking they hiss, and they are so fierce that they have the same place in the canine world as their masters have among mankind.

The men pierce the cartilage of the nose and ears, from which they hang various small ornaments. They make scars on their arms and chests with a very sharp iron instrument, which they whet on their teeth as on a stone. Their teeth are filed down nearly to the gums, and for this operation they use a rounded, tongue-shaped grindstone. They paint their faces and bodies in a frightful manner with a mixture of seal oil, ocher, soot, and plumbago. On festive occasions, they let their hair hang, powdered, and braided with the down of seabirds. They wear a pelt over their shoulders and nothing at all on the rest of the body except the head, which is usually covered with a small, skillfully woven straw hat. Sometimes, undoubtedly to appear more fearful to their enemies, they wear caps mounted with two horns and eagle feathers, or even whole bear heads within which they fit wooden headpieces.

Some savages wear otter-skin shirts, and the usual garment of a great chief is a shirt of tanned elk hide, fringed with deer hoofs and bird beaks which would rattle when he danced. La Pérouse saw tattooing on the arms of only some women. The women have a practice which makes them hideous; every one, without exception, has the lower lip split at the level of the gum along the entire width of the mouth; there they wear a kind of small wooden bowl which rests against the gum; the split lip forms a ring around the outside of the bowl in such a way that the lower part of the mouth juts out two or three inches. Young girls have only a needle in the lower lip, since the labret is the exclusive right of married women. The French often urged them to discard this ornament, but their honor seemed to depend on it, since they either refused or were distressed when they removed it. In the latter case, the lower lip fell upon the chin and they looked as grotesque as before. Dressed as they are in evil-smelling, untanned skins, these women are the most repulsive in the world.

The natives of Frenchmen's Harbor bear no resemblance to the Eskimos, to whom it was formerly believed they were related. They are much taller and thinner, not so hardy, and less skilled in building canoes, which they make by hollowing out a tree trunk and placing a board on each side for gunwales. Their line-fishing they do rather ingeniously: to each line they attach a large seal bladder which they leave on the water; each canoe puts out twelve to fifteen lines; when a fish is caught it drags along the bladder, and the canoe comes after it. In this way, two men can watch twelve to fifteen lines without the monotony of hand-tending them.

These people have made much more material than moral progress. Their arts are much more advanced than those of the South Sea islanders. They know how to forge iron, work copper, spin the wool of certain animals, and with this yarn to knit fabrics comparable to our tapestry. Nowhere are hats and baskets of rushes woven with greater skill. They sculpt human and animal figures in wood or stone moderately well. They are also able to cut jewels out of serpentine and polish them to the luster of marble.

We have already spoken of their passion for gambling. The game which generally sends them into a frenzy is based entirely on chance. They use

Indians at Frenchmen's Harbor on the northwest coast of America

thirty small pieces of wood, each of which, like our dice, has various marks. Seven of these are hidden. Each player has his turn, and whoever comes nearest to the number marked on the seven hidden pieces wins the prize, which is usually a lump of iron or a hatchet. This addiction to gambling makes them morose and uneasy. Nevertheless, La Pérouse often heard them sing. The chief who came to visit him usually sang when going around the ship, at the same time extending his arms in the shape of a cross as a sign of friendship; he then climbed aboard and there acted out a pantomime which expressed either a battle, or a surprise, or a death. The tune which preceded this performance was pleasant and quite harmonious. One final stroke to complete the picture of these people—they are cannibals. La Pérouse states that he did not observe among them any trace of this brutal custom, but the report of John Meares,[2] an English captain, proves conclusively that these natives are, in this respect, no better than the other savages of the northwest coast of America.

---

[2] Captain John Meares built a post at Nootka Sound in 1788 for trade with China. It was seized and held by Spain, 1789–1795. Meares named Mount Olympus in 1788 and discovered Juan de Fuca Strait in the same year.

CHAPTER IV

Departure from Frenchmen's Harbor
Exploration of the American Coast
Arrival and Stay at Monterey, California

LA PÉROUSE finally left these dismal shores on July 30, 1786, in order to continue his exploration of the American coast. The new voyage did not begin auspiciously; the fog, the rain, and the calm continued until about noon, August 4. On that day the mists disappeared and there was perfect visibility to the entrance of Cross Sound, where the snowcapped mountains reach down to the sea. The seacoast at this point, although the elevation is over five thousand feet, is covered with trees, even at the highest levels. At sunset La Pérouse raised the western point of Cross Sound, with Mount Fairweather and Mount Crillon to the northwest of him. Mount Crillon, almost as high as Mount Fairweather,[1] is north of Cross Sound, while Mount Fairweather is north of Frenchmen's Harbor. Because of their proximity, these peaks are the landmarks of the bay. On August 5, they raised a cape south of the entrance into Cross Sound and called it Cross Cape. The same day they sighted Cook's Bay of Islands.

During the following days, they learned that south of Cape Angano[2] the American coast is fringed with numerous islands for a distance of more than ten leagues and the continent lies far behind these islands. Between the islands and the mainland they believed there must be good harbors and

---

[1] Mount Fairweather is 15,320 feet high; Mount Crillon, 12,736 feet.
[2] Cook's Cape Edgecumbe.—Valentin

fine bays. La Pérouse named one of these bays Chirikof Bay, in honor of the famous Russian navigator who coasted this part of America in 1741. The same day, in the evening, he sighted a group of five small islands separated from the continent by a channel four or five leagues wide; these he named the La Croyère Islands, after the French geographer Lisle de la Croyère, who sailed with Captain Chirikof and died during the voyage.

From the 56th parallel to 53°, the sea was covered with a species of diver named, by Buffon, the Kamchatka black diver. The bird's body is black, its beak and feet are red, and on its head are two white stripes which rise in tufts like that of a cockatoo. It never goes more than five or six leagues from land and, when sighted, is a fairly certain sign that land is no farther than this.

On August 19, in the evening, they sighted a cape which forms the farthest point of the American coast. The visibility was excellent, and beyond this point only four or five small islands could be seen. These were named the Kerouart Islands [Queen Charlotte Islands]; the point was named Cape Hector.[3] This was the end of the coast which they had followed for two hundred leagues. La Pérouse turned northward in order to observe the other side of the land which he had just coasted to the east. He passed about a league from the Kerouart Islands and Cape Hector, then crossed powerful currents which forced him off course and away from the coast. During the night he was unable to make suitable progress, and he tacked until daybreak when he resumed the course of the day before. He observed the other side of La Touche Bay, which he named Cape Buache, and more than twenty leagues of the east coast along which he had sailed during the preceding days.

On August 24, he sighted a group of low islands, without trees or bushes, although the coast was covered with grass and driftwood. He named these the Sartine Islands.[4] On the 25th, he continued on a course eastward to the entrance of Nootka Sound. At five o'clock in the evening, a very dense fog

---

[3] Dixon's Cape St. James.—Valentin [Captain George Dixon, R.N., has been credited with discovering the Queen Charlotte Islands in 1787. He named them for his ship.]

[4] Gabriel de Sartine, Count of Alby (1729–1801), was a French statesman. Born in Barcelona, he became a police chief and later Minister of the Navy.

made it impossible to see land, and he steered a course toward the point of the breakers, fifteen leagues south of Nootka, in order to observe the section of the coast between Cape Flattery and the point of the breakers which Captain Cook had not been able to explore. This is a stretch of about thirty leagues.

On September 5, the ships were at 42° 58′ 56″ north latitude and 127° 5′ 20″ west longitude, passing among nine small islands or bare rocks which were named the Necker Islands.[5] They continued to follow the coast. Three or four leagues away mountaintops appeared above the clouds; the summits were covered with trees, and no snow was visible. At nightfall, the coast extended toward the southeast, but the lookouts were sure they had seen land south one-quarter southeast. Uncertain of the direction of the coast, which had never been explored, La Pérouse lightened his sails and made his course south-southwest. At daybreak they still saw land extending in a direction between north and north one-quarter northwest. They steered southeast one-quarter east in order to approach land, but, at seven o'clock in the morning of September 6, a dense fog blotted it out of sight. They found the sky less clear in this part of America than in the high latitudes where the navigators, at least part of the time, enjoyed the view of everything above their horizon. Here the visibility was always limited.

On September 7, the fog was even thicker than it had been the previous day; however, toward noon it cleared, and the mountaintops far to the east became visible. At the top of one of these mountains they saw a flaming volcano, but a dense fog soon deprived the navigators of this spectacle, and it was again necessary to leave the coast. Fearing that by following a course parallel to the shore he might run upon an island or a rock some distance from the mainland, La Pérouse stood out to sea.

On September 13, the land was sighted through the mists, but it was impossible to make any observations. When they approached to within one league of the shore, the breakers were seen very clearly. At nightfall they again stood out to sea and at daybreak bore back toward the land, with a

---

[5] Jacques Necker (1732–1804), born at Geneva, was a French banker and Minister of Finance. His fiscal reforms of 1777 and 1788 failed, and he recommended calling the Estates Général.

dense fog which cleared at midday. They then followed the coastline closely, and at three o'clock in the afternoon they sighted the Spanish fort[6] at Monterey and two three-masted ships which were in the roadstead. Opposing winds forced the frigates to anchor two leagues out; the following day they moored two cable-lengths from shore.

Monterey Bay, formed by Ano Nuevo Point on the north and Point Pinos on the south, is eight leagues wide and indents the low, sandy coast almost six leagues eastward. The sound of the sea, rolling in upon the foot of the sand dunes along the coast, can be heard more than a league away. North and south of the bay the land is high and covered with trees. It is difficult to imagine the number or familiarity of the whales surrounding the frigates. They spouted every minute, a half-pistol shot away, and filled the air with a foul odor. This phenomenon puzzled the French, but the local residents informed them that the water discharged by the cetaceans was impregnated with this evil smell which spread for a considerable distance. The sea was covered with pelicans. These birds, which never go more than five or six leagues from land, seemed to be very common along the entire California coast.

The natives of Monterey, small, thin, and colored somewhat like Negroes, are very adept archers. The French saw them hit the smallest birds. These they stalk with the most amazing patience; they hide and in some way creep toward the game, shooting only when they are about fifteen paces away. Their cunning in hunting deer is even more astounding. La Pérouse saw a savage, wearing the head of a buck upon his head, go on all fours, simulate grazing, and do this imitation so effectively that the French hunters would have shot him at thirty paces if they had not been previously informed of the ruse. In this way, the Indians stalk herds of deer and kill them with arrows at the shortest range.

Loreto, a small village with a fort, is the only presidio on the eastern shore of the peninsula of Lower California. The country is not healthful. The province of Sonora, which borders the Gulf of California on the east as Lower California does on the west, is certainly more attractive. This region has a fertile soil and productive mines, much more valuable assets

---

[6] Completed in 1778.

than the pearl fisheries of the peninsula, which require a certain number of slaves as divers, people who often are very difficult to obtain. Upper California, however, provides its inhabitants with many more of the factors of prosperity. Its oldest establishment, San Diego, dates only from 1769; it is the southernmost presidio, while San Francisco is the northernmost. These presidios or missions are the product of Spanish piety, since the Spaniards established them for the sole purpose of converting and civilizing the natives of these regions. The healthfulness of the air, the fertility of the earth, and last but not least, the abundance of every species of fur-bearing animal, which assures a profitable trade with China, have given this part of America an infinite advantage over Lower California, whose unhealthful climate and sterile ground cannot be compensated by a few pearls which have to be torn from the bottom of the sea. No country has a greater abundance of fish and game of every kind. All the aquatic birds are found in the greatest numbers on the ponds and the seacoast. The earth is incredibly productive. It is perfect for growing vegetables. The harvests of corn, barley, wheat, and peas can be compared only with those of Chile. The average return on wheat is about seventy-five to one. Finally, the climate is very similar to that of the provinces of southern France.

The earth, although excellent for vegetables, is light and sandy and owes its fertility to the dampness of the atmosphere. The nearest stream is two leagues from the presidio. Named Carmel River by the earliest explorers, this river flows past San Carlos Mission,[7] providing the missionaries and the savages with healthy, pleasant drinking water. With only a little labor, it can be used to irrigate the mission's gardens.

As already mentioned, on the evening of September 14, the frigates anchored two leagues out, in sight of the presidio and two ships which were in the roadstead. The next day they got under way at ten o'clock in the morning and at noon moored in this same roadstead. There they received a seven-cannon salute, which they returned, and La Pérouse sent an officer to the governor with the Spanish minister's letter which had been

---

[7] Founded at Monterey, on June 3, 1770, by Fr. Junipero Serra and moved almost immediately to Carmel Valley when Fr. Junipero built the church in which his remains have rested since his death on August 28, 1784.

delivered to him before he left France. It was unsealed and addressed to the viceroy of Mexico, whose jurisdiction extended as far as Monterey, even though the presidio was eleven hundred leagues distant from the capital.

The commander of the fort of both Californias gave the French the same welcome as if they had been his fellow countrymen; this chivalrous officer combined noble manners with the most liberal conduct. He sent beef, vegetables, and milk to the frigates' crews; his house soon became theirs, and he placed all of his servants at their disposal.

The fathers of San Carlos Mission, two leagues distant from Monterey, soon arrived at the presidio. These apostolic men, who had left the peaceful life of the cloister for every kind of hardship, care, and worry, showed themselves as kind to the strangers as had the officers of the fort and of the ships, and invited them to dine at the mission. The travelers accepted this invitation eagerly, and were received like lords making their first visit to their domains. The president of the mission, wearing his cope, awaited them at the door of the church, which was illuminated as brightly as on the greatest feast day; he conducted them to the foot of the main altar where he chanted the *Te Deum* in thanksgiving for the happy outcome of their voyage.

Before entering the church, the travelers had passed through a square where the savages of both sexes had formed a line; the savages' faces did not express any astonishment. The church, although it was thatched, was very clean. It was dedicated to St. Charles and decorated with a suitable number of good paintings, copies of Italian originals, among which the travelers noticed scenes of heaven and hell especially calculated to impress new converts. After leaving the church, the French again passed the line of Indians, who had not left their places; only the children had wandered off a little and formed groups near the missionaries' house. The huts of these savages are the most wretched to be found among any people. Eight or ten bundles of straw arranged on stakes driven into the ground give the Indians indifferent protection from the rain and the wind; more than half the hut is left uncovered when the weather is good. Despite the missionaries' admonitions, it has never been possible to change this type of structure which is generally used in Upper and Lower California; the savages reply that they like fresh air, that it is convenient to set fire to one's home when it has become infested with too much vermin and to be able to build another in less than a couple of hours.

The color of these natives, which is that of Negroes, the friars' house, their storehouses built of brick and stuccoed, the threshing-floor where they tread the wheat, the cattle, the horses—all these reminded the travelers of a settlement in Santo Domingo. As in that colony, the men and women assemble when the bell rings, and a friar leads them to work, to church, and to all other activities. By their replies to the various questions put to them, the friars explained how they, the spiritual and temporal authorities, rule this type of religious community. This is how the report described it:

"The Indians as well as the missionaries rise at daybreak and go to prayer and mass, which last about an hour. During this time, barley meal, which had been made by roasting the grains before grinding them, is cooked in three large kettles in the center of the square; this type of porridge, which the natives call *atole* and like very much, is not seasoned either with butter or with salt. Breakfast lasts three-quarters of an hour, after which all of them go to work. Some till the ground with oxen, others dig in the garden; each one serves the different needs of the community, and all are under the supervision of one or two friars. The women are occupied caring for their households and children, and roasting and grinding grain. This last is a lengthy and difficult task because the women have only a roller for crushing grain against a stone. After witnessing this operation, Captain de Langle gave his mill to the missionaries. He had another windmill made for the frigates, and this one was used for the rest of the cruise.

"At noon the bells announce dinner. At two o'clock, the work is resumed and continues until five. Next comes the evening prayer, which lasts nearly an hour. After this prayer, another ration of *atole*, equal to the breakfast portion, is distributed.

"Individuals are paid with small amounts of grain from which the savages make small, thin cakes, cooking them under the embers. On feast days there is a ration of beef. They are often permitted to hunt and fish for themselves, and when they return, they usually make the missionaries some presents of fish and game. They have never been known to steal from one another, although the only way they close an empty hut is by placing a single bundle of straw across the entrance.

"The Christian Indians have kept all their old customs not forbidden by their new religion: the same huts, the same games, the same clothing. They also paint themselves black when in mourning. The missionaries have to permit this practice because these people are deeply attached to their friends. For them, family ties are not so strong as those of friendship. Children hardly know their father; they leave his hut as soon as they are able to obtain their own food. Of much greater duration is their attachment to their mother, who raises them with the greatest gentleness, thrashing them only when they show cowardice in their little fights with children their own age.

"The old men who are no longer able to hunt are supported by the whole village and are highly respected. Outside of the missions, the savages are frequently at war, but their fear of the Spanish makes them respect the missions. They do not practice cannibalism habitually; however, when they have conquered and killed brave men or chiefs in battle, they eat some parts of them, not as a sign of hatred and revenge but rather in homage to the victims' valor and in the belief that this food will enhance their own courage. They remove the scalps of their victims and take out the eyes, which they are able to preserve and which they prize as evidence of their victories. It is their custom to burn the dead and to place their ashes in *marae* (tombs). They have no knowledge of God or a hereafter, with the exception of some of the southern tribes who had an obscure notion of this before the arrival of the missionaries. They set their paradise in the midst of the ocean where the elect enjoy, according to their belief, a cool climate such as they never have on their burning sands; hell they believe is in the bowels of the mountains."[8]

---

[8] Since La Pérouse wrote these lines, considerable changes have taken place in the two Californias. These provinces participated in the rebellion which separated Spanish America from the mother country. Nevertheless, the missionaries, who have dedicated their lives to helping and civilizing these people deep in the darkness of ignorance, are continuing their evangelical work in these regions. Today the two Californias are part of the Mexican Union, although without enjoying the advantages of member states. The capital of the area is the little city of Monterey, whose population is less than one thousand and whose harbor is far from deserving the importance which the Spanish have tried to give it.—Valentin

Northern or New California, whose northernmost settlement is San Francisco, is bounded only by the limits of North America. When the French frigates went as far as Mount St. Elias, they still had not reached these limits. All along the coast the amphibious otter, so prized for its pelt, is as numerous as the seals on the coast of Labrador and Hudson Bay. The natives, who are not as expert sailors as the Eskimoes and whose boats are made only of rushes, lasso otters found on land and club those found on the water. For this purpose, they lie hidden behind rocks, since the slightest noise alarms the animal and it immediately dives.

Despite its fertility, New California still has only a small population. This is due partly to its great distance from Europe and partly to its system of government which, with certain exceptions, does not provide for private ownership of property and permits converted Indians to be only partially free.

From the day of their arrival, the French were busy taking on water and wood. For their part, the naturalists lost no time in adding to their botanical collection. The season, however, was not favorable; the plants had been completely dried by the summer heat and their seeds scattered over the earth. Nevertheless, the naturalists were able to study the sea wormwood, the great wormwood, Mexican tea, southernwood, mugwort, starwort, Canadian goldenrod, yarrow, the black nightshade, samphire, and water-mint. The gardens of the governor and of the Franciscan missionaries were filled with countless pot-herbs, which the sailors gathered.

La Pérouse wished to pay for the services of the Spanish soldiers by giving them each a piece of blue cloth. To the mission he sent blankets, cloth, beads, and in general all the small articles they needed. On September 22, he took leave of the commandant, the missionaries, and the natives who had given his crews such a pleasant reception. The same evening, after all had come aboard, the ships were ready to set sail. They were as well supplied now as when they left Concepcion.

CHAPTER V

Voyage from Monterey to Macao
Stop in Macao Bay—Arrival in Manila
Description of Luzon

WHEN HE LEFT MONTEREY, La Pérouse planned to steer a course to the southwest, in order to reach the Mariana Islands. The crossing was at first very pleasant, but on October 18 the winds came from the west and persisted as stubbornly as in the high latitudes. The ships struggled against this opposition for eight to ten days; the rain and storms almost never stopped. Because of the extreme dampness between-decks, all of the sailors' gear was wet, and the commander feared that adverse conditions would lead to an outbreak of scurvy. On November 4, they sighted a small island at 24° 4′ north latitude and 165° 2′ west longitude. It is no more than a rock, about one thousand yards long and at the most one hundred twenty-five yards high.[1] Not a single tree was visible, but there was plenty of grass at the top. La Pérouse came within a third of a league of the island; the shores, standing against the breaking might of the sea, are as perpendicular as a wall. To disembark there was absolutely out of the question. This place was named Necker Island.

During this day, lookouts were continuously at the mastheads. The weather was squally with rain, nevertheless, La Pérouse ordered all the studding sails to be taken in and the frigates' speed reduced to three or four miles an hour. The winds were easterly, the course west. At about

---

[1] Actual elevation is 277 feet.

half past one in the morning, breakers were seen two cable lengths ahead of the frigates. The sea was so calm that the waves made hardly any noise and only rolled out at great intervals. The two captains immediately swung hard-a-port, heading south-southeast. They managed to avoid the danger by the narrowest possible margin. The least inadvertence in carrying out the maneuvers necessary to miss these reefs would certainly have resulted in the loss of the two vessels, but everything was done in an orderly and efficient manner.

It was not enough for La Pérouse to have avoided the danger; he did not want the navigators who would sail this sea after him to be exposed to it. Consequently, at daybreak, he approached the reef and sighted a small island or split rock, about three hundred feet in diameter and about one hundred forty feet high.[2] Between the islet and the breakers to the south he saw three sand banks which are not more than four feet above the level of the seas. They are separated from each other by greenish water which does not appear to be one fathom deep. Level with the water a ring of rocks surrounds the shoal, like diamonds circling a medal, and protects it from the pounding fury of the sea. These banks, which almost terminated the voyage of our navigators, were named French Frigate Shoal.

La Pérouse next sailed west-southwest, hoping finally to find some land of importance in that direction. He expected Necker Island and French Frigate Shoal to be part of an archipelago which was inhabited or at least inhabitable. His expectations, however, were not realized; soon the birds, those harbingers of land, disappeared entirely and with them all hope of any discovery.

The voyage continued uneventfully until December 14, when they approached the Mariana Islands. They soon sighted Assumption [Asuncion], one of the numerous islands of this archipelago. The most melancholy imagination would have difficulty visualizing so dreadful a place. After such a long crossing, the appearance of the most ordinary land should have delighted the French sailors. However, a perfect cone of a frightful black color, rising two hundred fifty feet above the surface of the sea,

---

[2] La Pérouse Pinnacle, elevation 122 feet.

only dashed their hopes after several weeks of anticipating the turtles and coconuts which they would find in the Marianas.

The frigates, however, dropped anchor a short distance from the island. Two boats, commanded by de Langle and Boutin, approached the land. These two officers had considerable difficulty getting ashore. The sea was breaking everywhere, and they had to wait for an opportunity between the breakers to leap into the water up to their necks. After returning, they reported that the island was even more dreadful than it at first appeared, with nothing but lava flows and precipices edged with a few stunted coconut palms. After pouring out of a crater, the lava had covered the entire cone and the surrounding area for a distance of about two hundred fifty feet toward the sea. The summit looked as if it had been vitrified, and the glass was as black as soot. Although no smoke was visible, the pervasive odor of sulphur definitely proved that the volcano was not extinct. All the evidence indicated that no human beings and no quadrupeds had ever been so unfortunate as to have been required to live in this desolate place.

Again setting sail, the frigates followed a course of west one-quarter northwest. Between the Mariana Islands and the Philippines, the winds were brisk, the sea very high, and the currents continually bore to the south. On December 28, they sighted the Bashi Islands.[3] They passed about one league from the two great rocks which are the northernmost part of this group. La Pérouse did not wish to stop in this archipelago which had been visited many times and had nothing of interest to offer. After determining the position of these islands, he continued on his way to China, and on January 1, 1787, he sounded bottom at sixty fathoms. The next day, the vessels were surrounded by a great number of deep-sea fishing boats; these appeared to pay no attention to the strangers. Their piscatorial technique did not permit them to turn aside to greet the frigates; they drag the bottom with extremely long nets which take more than two hours to raise.

On January 2, the French sighted the White Stone. In the evening they moored to the north of Ling-ting Island and on the next day were in the

---

[3] The Batan Islands, northernmost part of the Philippines.

roadstead of Macao. Chinese pilots had been taken on just inside of Lamma Island. The weather was so overcast that the French could not see the city, but it cleared at noon, and they raised the city to the west, one degree south, at about three leagues. La Pérouse sent to shore a boat commanded by Lieutenant Boutin, to inform the governor of his arrival and of his intention to remain in the roadstead until his crew was rested and refreshed. Don Bernardo Alexis de Lemos, governor of Macao, received the officer most kindly; he offered the expedition all the assistance at his disposal and immediately sent a Moorish pilot to guide the French to the Taipa anchorage. At sunrise the next day the frigates got under way and dropped anchor in Macao next to a ship of the French navy, the *Maréchal de Castries*, which was cruising the shores of the Orient with the mission of protecting our commerce. Thus, after eighteen months of hardship at sea, our sailors had the pleasure of meeting not only their own countrymen but also friends and fellow servicemen.

After mooring the frigates by head and stern, the commander's first task was to go ashore with Captain de Langle to ask the governor for permission to establish a shore base where they could set up an observatory and an infirmary for Dagelet the astronomer and Rollin the ship's doctor, who had been exhausted by the voyage. Don Bernardo Lemos received them as his own countrymen and granted all their requests with the greatest courtesy. His home was open to them and, as he did not speak French, his wife, a young Portuguese from Lisbon, served him as interpreter. To her husband's cooperation, she added a charm which was quite her own and which the visitors could expect to meet with only very infrequently in the great cities of Europe.

After all the travelers who have written about China, we will not stop here to record the comments of La Pérouse concerning this country; comments, moreover, which after the passage of fifty years have lost much of their accuracy and relevance. We will limit our remarks to Macao, ceded in perpetuity to the Portuguese in about 1580.

No longer the prosperous city made wealthy when its owners enjoyed a near monopoly in the trade with Japan, Tonkin, and other countries of eastern Asia, today it has a population of about 15,000. The Chinese regard Canton as the refuge of the worst people of neighboring nations

View of Macao

and Macao as the cesspool of Canton. As a matter of fact, its population consists of Chinese, most of whom have escaped from prisons, Malays, and Portuguese mulattoes who have all the vices of their ancestors without any of their virtues. Situated at the mouth of the Tigre, the city has a roadstead at the entrance to Taipa, which can receive 64-gun warships, and a harbor which can accommodate vessels of seven or eight hundred tons loaded to half their capacity. The harbor entrance is guarded by a fortress containing two batteries; entering ships must pass within a pistol-shot of these. Three small forts secure the northern sector of the city against any Chinese attack. Furthermore, commanding the beach is a mountain on which troops could withstand a prolonged siege. The Portuguese have built a church upon the ruins of a fort which crowned the mountain and provided an impregnable position. Landwards the defenses consist of two fortresses which overlook the entire countryside. The Portuguese frontier is scarcely a league from the city; along it is a wall guarded by a mandarin and some soldiers. This Chinese official is the actual governor of Macao, whom the Chinese residents obey. He does not have the right to reside within the limits of Macao, but he can visit the town and even the fortifications and inspect the customs. On these occasions, the Portuguese owe him a five-gun salute. No European, however, can set foot on the Chinese soil beyond the wall.

Since it was impossible to get his damaged ships repaired at Macao, La Pérouse decided to go to Manila, where resources of every kind were available. Consequently, after a month's stay, he left the mouth of the Tigre, taking with him three marines from the *Maréchal de Castries* and six Chinese sailors on each frigate to replace the men whom he had the misfortune to lose at Frenchmen's Harbor. On February 15, he sighted the island of Luzon. Since unfavorable currents prevented him from entering the bay, he decided to stop in the harbor of Mariveles, there to await either better winds or a more favorable current. Because he needed wood or knew that it was expensive in Manila, he decided to remain in this village for twenty-four hours in order to take on a supply. At dawn the next day, all the carpenters of both frigates were sent ashore in long-boats. The commander likewise went ashore. Mariveles consists of about forty houses which are constructed of bamboo, covered with leaves, and raised four or five feet above the ground. The floors of these houses are made of small bamboos which are not joined and thus cause these cabins somewhat to resemble bird cages. Entry is by a ladder, and all the material in such a house, including the roofing, does not weigh more than two hundred pounds. The population of the village consists of about two hundred natives of both sexes and all ages, under the direction of a curate. They are always ready, at the slightest alarm, to flee into the woods in order to escape Moros who make frequent raids upon their coast. At the time of La Pérouse's visit, the spiritual care of these unfortunate people was entrusted to a young native mulatto whose evangelical simplicity was reminiscent of the days of the early Church; he lived in a kind of hovel furnished only with some earthen pots and a pallet.

At daybreak on February 25, they set sail and approached Manila Bay from the south. Finally on February 28, they moored in the harbor of Cavite, dropping anchor two cable lengths from the town. An officer of the town's commandant immediately came on board to request the strangers not to communicate with the shore until the arrival of orders from the governor-general, to whom he would dispatch a messenger as soon as he learned why the frigates had stopped there. La Pérouse replied that he wanted victuals and permission for his crew to rest in order to continue with his expedition as quickly as possible. Before the Spanish officer could leave, the bay commander arrived from Manila, from where the ships had been observed. Lieutenant Boutin left in this officer's boat to call upon the governor-general, who received him graciously and granted the French whatever they possibly needed. He was even so kind as to write to the commandant at Cavite to ask him to allow the travelers to enter the town and to provide them with all the assistance and accommodations available there. From then on, they were virtually citizens of Cavite. The ships were so close to the shore that the crew could disembark and go back on board at any and all times. Various buildings were obtained for working on the sails, salting provisions, constructing two boats, and lodging the naturalists and geographers. The commandant was generous enough to lend his own home for the establishment of the observatory. No restrictions whatever were placed on the travelers' freedom of action, and in the market and the arsenal they found the same supplies as in the best harbors of Europe.

View of Cavite in Manila Bay

Prao, *a Philippine coasting vessel*

Sarambo, *a Philippine fishing net*

Cavite, three leagues south of Manila, was formerly a quite important town, but in the Philippines, as in Europe, the big cities somehow absorb the little ones. As in La Pérouse's time, Cavite today is a town where the only Spaniards are the government officials and the arsenal supervisors. The population, consisting of natives and people of mixed ancestry, is not more than 6,000; the harbor, which is as safe as that of Manila, serves as a refuge for vessels during the monsoons.

The second day after their arrival in Cavite, La Pérouse and Captain de Langle, accompanied by several officers, took a boat to Manila. Two and a half hours were required to make this trip. There are no pleasanter views than those which they enjoyed during this crossing. First they called upon the governor, who invited them to dinner and gave them his captain of the guards to take them to the archbishop and the intendant.

The city of Manila or Luzon, including its suburbs, is quite large, with an estimated population of 38,000,[4] among whom are scarcely 1,000 to 1,200 Spaniards. The other inhabitants are mixed, natives, and Chinese. They cultivate all the arts and produce goods of every kind. The country around the city is enchanting. A beautiful river, the Pasig or Manila, winds through it and is divided into several canals, of which the two largest lead into the famous Laguna de Bay, a lake situated seven leagues in the interior and surrounded by more than a hundred native villages, where the soil is the most fertile imaginable.

Manila, built upon pilings because of the frequent earthquakes, is one of the most pleasantly situated cities in the world. It occupies a fertile plain on the west coast of the island, at the end of the bay which bears its name. The streets are broad, straight, lined with sidewalks, and paved with granite imported from China. The most important buildings are the churches and convents, and the palace of the governor. Cigars and gold chains are the leading commercial products of the inhabitants.

More than three million people inhabit the Philippine archipelago. These people are in no way inferior to Europeans; they cultivate their land skillfully; they are honest, hospitable, courteous, and in no way

---

[4] This number, as well as that of the population of the Philippine Islands, has more than doubled since La Pérouse's time.—Valentin

deserve the contempt with which the Spaniards speak of them. The most repulsive distinctions between the natives and the Europeans have been established and are maintained with the greatest severity. Their extreme grievances have often led the natives to rebel without, however, destroying the happy influence which the climate has had on them. The country-people still have a cheerful manner, which can be found in very few European villages. Their homes are admirably clean and shaded by fruit trees which grow without cultivation.

These people are so excessively fond of tobacco that there is not a moment in the day when the men, and even the women, do not have cigars in their mouths. Children hardly out of the cradle form this habit. Luzon tobacco is the best in Asia. Cotton, indigo, sugar cane, and coffee spring up, one might say, underfoot, unheeded by the natives. Their spices are as excellent as those of the Moluccas.[5]

La Pérouse remained in Manila only a few hours; at eight o'clock in the evening he was back on board the frigate. The great heat of these latitudes began to have a disastrous effect upon his crews' health, and symptoms of dysentery were already becoming evident on board the frigates. Ensign d'Aigremont, who had caught the germ of this dread disease at Macao, died after an illness of twenty-five days.

---

[5] The island of Luzon is divided into two parts, one of which is independent and the other under Spanish rule. The former is inhabited by various tribes, some of which are savage; that of the Aetas is the most numerous. These tribes, who have lived in the mountains and the densest forest since the Malays established themselves on the island, belong to the Negro race. They occupy part of the eastern coast and almost all of the interior.—Valentin

CHAPTER VI

Departure from Cavite
The Island of Formosa—Entry into the Sea of Japan
Landing on the Coast of Tartary

ON MARCH 28 all the work at Cavite was completed; the boats were built, the sails repaired, the rigging inspected, the frigates completely caulked, and the salt provisions barrelled. On April 9, after paying his calls and expressing his thanks, the French captain set sail with a good northeast breeze which led him to believe that he could double all the islands in the entrance of Manila Bay before nightfall. As soon as he had doubled Cape Bojador, the wind steadied from the northeast so persistently that the northward progress of the frigates was slowed considerably. On April 21, they sighted the island of Formosa [Taiwan]; on the following days, foul weather forced the ships away from the coast, and for two days they sailed over an immense bank where they were sounding the bottom continuously. Their tack brought them back to the coast of Formosa near the entrance to the ancient Fort Zealand,[1] at the city of Taiwan [Tainan], capital of the island. La Pérouse was informed of the rebellion in the colony and understood that an army of 20,000 men, commanded by the santon of Canton, had been sent against the rebels. Since the force of the northeast monsoon was still undiminished, the French commander had the satisfaction of being able to devote several days to learning the latest developments in the rebellion, and he anchored west of Taiwan Bay.

---

[1] Constructed by the Dutch in 1624.

Uncertain whether he should send ashore a boat, which could easily rouse suspicions in view of the war which was going on in the colony, he decided to try to get the attention of some Chinese who were sailing nearby; he showed them some piastres, which he thought would be a powerful lure for these people, but they were probably forbidden to have any communication with foreigners. They obviously were not afraid of the French, since they passed within range of their weapons, but they refused to come alongside. Only one had nerve; the French bought his fish at the price he quoted. It was impossible to understand this fisherman's answers to the questions which they asked him and which he certainly did not comprehend. Not only did these people's language have nothing in common with that of the Europeans, but the kind of sign language believed to be universal was no better understood. This fruitless effort convinced La Pérouse of the uselessness of sending a boat ashore and of the impossibility of satisfying his curiosity.

The next day, the breeze off shore and on the sea having permitted the frigates to move ten leagues farther north, they sighted the Chinese army at the mouth of a large river at 23° 25′ north latitude, where the banks are four or five leagues apart. They came to anchor opposite this river, in thirty-seven fathoms, a mud bottom. It was impossible to count the Chinese ships which were in sight; some were under sail, others were moored at the water's edge, and a great number of them were in the river. The flagship, covered with divers pennants, was farthest out to sea; it was anchored at the edge of the shoal water, a league east of the French frigates. As soon as night fell, lights were hung on all of its masts to direct several ships which were still before the wind. These ships had to pass close by the *Boussole* and the *Astrolabe* in order to join their commander, and they were very careful not to approach within extreme cannon range of them, being obviously uncertain whether the frigates were friend or foe.

La Pérouse raised the southern islands of the Pescadores on a bearing of west one-quarter northwest; it was probable that the Chinese army, after leaving the province of Fukien, had assembled at the island of Penghu, the most important of this group. La Pérouse was still unable to satisfy his curiosity, since the weather had become stormy. Insuperable difficulties caused him to return to the south of Formosa, in order to sail along the east side of this island. It was clear to him that before the monsoon changed he would never succeed in steering a course through the channel.[2] Forced to adopt this expedient, he at least wanted to reconnoiter the Pescadores Islands to the extent permitted by the bad weather. He sailed along the southernmost ones at a distance of two leagues and located them at a latitude of 23° 12′.

These islands are a mass of rocks which have taken all kinds of shapes; one of them looks exactly like the Cordouan lighthouse, located at the mouth of the Bordeaux River,[3] and one could swear that this rock had been hewn by human hands. These islets seem to be absolutely barren. The next day the frigates went through a fierce squall preceded by one of those heavy downpours which occur only in the tropics. The lightning continued throughout the night; the flashes came from all directions, and yet only one clap of thunder was heard.

The ships remained in a dead calm throughout the next day, midway between the Batan Islands and Botol-Taboco-Shima. After the winds permitted them to come within two or three leagues of the latter, three villages were clearly visible on the southern coast. La Pérouse wished that he could visit these villages, whose inhabitants had been described by Dampier[4] as honest and hospitable, but the only bay which seemed to provide a convenient anchorage was open to the southeast winds which were beginning to blow steadily. After doubling this island, the frigates were, therefore, forced to follow a course northeast. On May 5 at one o'clock in the morning, they sighted an island to the southwest. For the remainder of the night they tacked under light sails, and at daybreak followed a course on which they would pass a half league west of the island. It was soon obvious that the island was inhabited. Fires were

---

[2] Presumably the Pescadores Channel, which separates these islands from Formosa.

[3] The most famous lighthouse of the eighteenth century, the Cordouan lighthouse was located opposite the mouth of the Gironde River in the Bay of Biscay and marked the entrance to that river.

[4] William Dampier, a seventeenth-century buccaneer, wrote *A New Voyage Round the World* after travels across the North Pacific, in the East Indies, and to the northwest coast of Australia.

visible in several places, and herds of cattle were seen grazing along the coast. Several canoes took off from the shore in order to watch the frigates at less distance; the men who were in them seemed terrified at the sight of strangers. The shouts of the French sailors, however, and their motions and peaceful signs led two of the canoes to come alongside. La Pérouse ordered that each be given a length of nankeen and some medals. It was evident that the islanders had not left their shore with the intention of doing any trading since they had nothing to offer in exchange for the gifts which they received, and they tied a bucket of fresh water to a line while making signs that they considered themselves in debt to the French. They invited the French to come close to land and tried to make them understand that they could have whatever they wanted there. These islanders are neither Chinese nor Japanese but, located between the two empires, seem to take after both nations. They dress in shirts and drawers of cotton cloth; their hair, tied up on the top of the head, is rolled around a gold pin; each one has a dagger, the handle of which also is fashioned of gold. Their canoes are made simply of hollowed-out trees, and they handle them rather poorly. La Pérouse would very much have liked to land on this island, but he had no time to lose, and it was important for him to be out of the Sea of Japan before the month of June, when storms and hurricanes make these waters the most dangerous in the world. For this place he kept the name Koumi Island, which it has on Father Gaubil's[5] map.

The expedition continued on its northward course under full sail, and by sunset Koumi Island was out of sight. At daybreak they sighted an island to the north-northwest and several rocks or islets farther to the east. They passed this island at a distance of a third of a league, without sounding the bottom, and saw nothing to indicate that it was inhabited. After they had passed it, they sighted a second island of the same size, also wooded and having the same general configuration as the first except

---

[5] Antoine Gaubil (1689–1759), born at Gaillac near Albi, was a French missionary and Chinese scholar, an author and rector of Pekin College. In 1704 he joined the Jesuit Order and in 1723 was sent to China. He translated the *Chou-King* (Paris 1771) and published *Histoire de Gentchiscan et de toute la dynastie des Manjoux* (Paris 1739), *Traité de Chronologie Chinoise* (Paris 1814), and other works.

that it was somewhat less escarped. These were the Hoa-Ponsu and Tiaoyu-Su Islands of Father Gaubil, which are located east of the northern end of Formosa. Finally, they were beyond the archipelago of the Ryūkyūs and were about to enter a much greater sea between Japan and China.

Off the China coast, La Pérouse encountered unfavorable conditions which prevented him from making more than seven or eight leagues a day. The fogs there were as thick and lasting as off the coast of Labrador. The ships were often becalmed, forced to anchor and to use signals to remain at anchor because they could not see one another even though they were within calling distance. The current was so strong that it was impossible for the plummet to sound bottom and to be certain that they were not running aground. The tide was changing continuously, and it moved around the compass exactly within twelve hours without leaving a single moment of slack water. On May 19, however, after a calm with a very dense fog which lasted fifteen days, a very brisk wind stood steady from the northwest; the weather remained cloudy and gray, but the visibility was several leagues. The sea, which had been so beautiful until then, began to run very high. La Pérouse, who was anchored in twenty-five fathoms at the time this wind began, immediately signaled to weigh anchor and, without losing a moment, set a course for Quelpart Island [Saishu To or Cheju Do], which was the first interesting place to be observed before entering Korea Strait. This island, which until then had not been inspected since shipwrecked Dutch sailors of the *Sparrow Hawk* were there in 1635, was under the jurisdiction of the king of Korea. The French sighted it on May 12, when the weather was perfect.

There is hardly another place which offers a more beautiful view: rising in the middle of the island to a height of over 6,000 feet is a peak which is visible from eighteen or twenty leagues and which undoubtedly is the source of the island's water supply. On land which slopes very gently down to the sea, the islanders' homes rise as if on the tiers of an amphitheater. The history of the shipwrecked Dutchmen who were kept captive on this place for eighteen years was not likely to prompt La Pérouse to send a boat ashore. He did see two canoes leave the shore, but they never came within a league of the frigates. Evidently their sole purpose was to observe the foreigners and perhaps to transmit a warning to the coast of Korea. The expedition, therefore, continued on its course. The next day they sighted various islands or rocks which form a chain more than fifteen leagues off the mainland of Korea. During the night of May 25, they passed through the Korea Strait, taking soundings every half hour.

The channel which separates Korea from Japan is about fifteen leagues wide. Since La Pérouse followed closely along the mainland, he could see the houses and towns on the seacoast. On some of the mountaintops he observed fortifications which exactly resembled European forts. These Korean defenses were obviously directed against the Japanese. The sight of the French frigates did not frighten a dozen sampans which were sailing along the coast. These sampans did not appear any different from those of the Chinese and had the same kind of mat sails. La Pérouse would have been happy to have the opportunity to communicate with them, but they continued on course without paying any attention to the foreign ships.

May 26 was one of the most beautiful days of the voyage and one of the most interesting, by reason of an occurrence which took place more than thirty leagues from shore. Despite the fine weather, this same day, nevertheless, brought a storm which was preceded by a remarkable phenomenon: from the top of the masts the lookouts shouted that they felt blasts of hot air coming every thirty seconds, as if from a furnace. All the officers climbed to the top of the masts and experienced the same heat. The temperature was then 14.° on the deck; a thermometer placed on the topgallant yard rose to 20°.[6] The blasts of heat, however, went by very rapidly, and the temperature of the intervening air was no different from that at the water's level.

On the next day, May 27, La Pérouse decided that he should steer a course for the southwest point of the island of Honshu. Soon he sighted, to the north-northeast, a small inhabited island which had not previously been on any map and which was named Dagelet Island [Ullung Do or Utsuryo-To], after the astronomer who first sighted it. The island is very

---

[6] On the Réaumur thermometric scale; the Fahrenheit equivalents are approximately 66° and 76°.

steep but is covered to the water's edge with the finest trees. Like a rampart, the sharp and almost perpendicular rock surrounds the entire island with the exception of some small sandy coves where it is possible to land. In these coves, they saw on the stocks some boats of Chinese design. The workmen, frightened by the sight of the frigates, fled into a neighboring forest. La Pérouse was eager to find an anchorage in order to prove to these people that he was not an enemy, but the current's force carried him away from land, and the fear of being brought to leeward made him give up his plan.

On the following days the winds continued to be contrary. On June 2 they passed within hail of two Japanese vessels; there were twenty-two crewmen aboard, all dressed in blue smocks which looked like the cassocks of Catholic priests. These ships, of about one hundred tons burden, had a single, very high mast and carried an immense sail. From all indications, they were not intended to go far from land, nor could they be safe in rough seas and a high wind. The frigates passed so close to one of these craft that the faces of those aboard were clearly visible, and they expressed neither fear nor surprise. The local vessels hurried away, no doubt in order to announce to their fellow countrymen the arrival of two foreign vessels in seas never before penetrated by European navigators.

On June 6 they raised Cape Noto on the west coast of Japan and Jootsi-Shima, an island separated from it by a channel about five leagues wide. The weather was clear and the visibility was perfect. Although six leagues from land, they could distinguish all the details of the shore—the trees, the streams, and the landslips. Some small islands or rocks, connected by lines of rocks which were just awash, prevented the frigates from coming closer to the shore. Jootsi-Shima is a small island, flat but well wooded and pleasing in appearance. Among the houses are some rather large buildings, and near a kind of castle there are some posts with a broad crossbeam which look exactly like our forked gibbets. Perhaps these posts have a different purpose; it would be quite exceptional if the Japanese, who are so different from Europeans, should agree with them on this point.

CHAPTER VII

Stops at Ternei, Suffren, De Langle,
* D'Estaing, and De Castries Bays*
Manners and Customs of the Tartars
Cape Krilon—Sakhalin Island
Arrival at Kamchatka

AFTER LA PÉROUSE observed Cape Noto on the western coast of Japan, he steered northwest in order to leave Japan, and on June 11, 1787, he sighted the mainland at twenty leagues' distance to the west, exactly at the boundary of Korea and Manchuria.[1] The land was very high and steep but covered with trees and greenery. They approached the coast until sounding bottom at eighty fathoms. The mountains are over four thousand feet high, their tops are covered with small amounts of snow. There were no visible indications that any civilized people lived there, nor were any rivers seen within a stretch of over forty leagues. The weather was perfect and the sky very clear. By June 14 they were already at 44.° latitude and had been able to correct the errors of the older maps. Fogs rolled in on them, and when the weather cleared on the 23rd La Pérouse dropped anchor in Ternei Bay, a half league from shore.

The configuration of the bay forms five small coves separated from each other by hills which are covered right up to their crests with trees. It was impossible to believe that so fertile a country, situated so near to China, could be uninhabited. As a matter of fact, signs of human beings were found at every step; several trees cut with sharp tools, hunting shelters built in the nooks of the forest, and little baskets made of stitched

---

[1] At this point the Tumen River empties into the Sea of Japan.

birch bark; finally, the destructive effects of fire were noticed in twenty places.

Some of the men went into the forest, but they killed only three fawns. By way of compensation, the fishing was very plentiful.

One day, a party coming to the edge of a brook discovered a tomb situated next to an abandoned cabin almost completely overgrown with weeds. When they opened the tomb, they found two well-preserved bodies lying side by side, wrapped in bearskin. Each had a belt from which hung some small Chinese coins and various copper ornaments. The corpses' heads were covered with taffeta caps. Blue glass beads were scattered about in the tomb where the explorers also found a dozen silver bracelets each weighing about a quarter of an ounce, a wooden spoon, a comb, a small blue nankeen bag filled with rice, an iron hatchet, and an iron knife. This tomb consisted merely of a small stack of logs covered with birch bark, with a space left in the center for the two bodies. The French were very careful to cover them again, religiously returning every article to its place, except for a very small selection of different objects which they took away from the tomb as evidence of their discovery. There was no longer any doubt that this region's nomadic inhabitants visited this bay frequently. A canoe left near the tomb indicated that they came here by sea.

On the morning of June 27, after depositing on shore various medals and also a bottle and an inscription to verify the date of their visit, the French set sail. "I followed the coast at a distance of two-thirds of a league," said La Pérouse. "From time to time we were able to make out the mouth of a small stream. Thus we covered fifty leagues in the finest weather a navigator could imagine. Then fogs and calms held us up until July 4. During this time we caught more than eight hundred codfish; what could not be eaten immediately was salted and placed in hogsheads. The dragnet also collected quite a large amount of oysters. Their shells were so fine that it seemed very possible they should have contained pearls, although we found only two partly formed pearls in the lot. This occurrence tended to confirm the report of the Jesuits who informed us that there were pearl fisheries at the mouths of several rivers in western Tartary."

The weather became quite clear on July 4, and a landing was made on the shore of a bay into which flows a river about one hundred feet wide. This place was named Suffren Bay.[2] Here the signs of human activity were much more recent than at the previous place, to which, moreover, this one bears a definite resemblance. On the 6th, the frigates had to struggle against contrary winds; on the morning of the 7th, being in 48° 50' latitude, La Pérouse sighted what appeared to be a large land mass to the east. No foreland could be seen but only some mountaintops which extend to the southeast, indicating that the expedition had already reached the channel which separates this land from the coast to the west. They stood to the eastward. There the land appears entirely different from Tartary. Only bare rocks could be seen, with some snow still in the hollows. They were not yet near enough to see the low land, which could be covered with trees and greenery as it is on the other side of the gulf.

Enveloped by fogs, the ships now had to grope their way through the channel, the configuration of which was unknown. Finally, on July 11, the weather cleared enough for the French to approach the strange land. They found it as well wooded as the coast of Tartary. They dropped anchor two miles from a small cove into which a river empties. With the help of their spyglasses, they sighted some cabins and two islanders who seemed to be fleeing into the forest. Two boats were on the shore; the houses had been abandoned only a short time before, since the fires were still burning. None of the furniture had been removed, and there was a litter of puppies whose eyes were not yet open. Their mother, barking in the woods, proved that the masters were not far away. Some hatchets as well as various iron tools and glass beads were left in these dwellings by the visitors, to prove that they were not enemies.

Just when they were about to return to the ships, a canoe carrying seven islanders approached the shore. They showed no sign of fearing the many Frenchmen, ran their small craft up on the beach, and sat down on two mats in the midst of the strangers, all with a serious, dignified,

---

[2] Pierre André de Suffren (1729–1788), born at St. Canat, Aix, was a French admiral who won renown fighting the English in Asian waters. He was a member of the Order of Malta.

and warmhearted manner. Among them were two very old men with long, white beards, clad in bark cloth similar to that worn by the natives of Madagascar. Two others wore blue quilted nankeen clothes, only slightly different in style from those worn by the Chinese. The others had only a long gown, which was closed by means of a belt and some small buttons. They go bareheaded, except for two or three who wear bearskin bands. Clean-shaven on face and front of the head, the hair on the back of their heads is kept eight or ten inches long. All have sealskin boots, the soles of which are made very artistically in the Chinese fashion. They are armed with pikes, bows, and iron-tipped arrows. The oldest of these men, to whom the others showed the greatest respect, had an eye disease which forced him to wear an eye-shade. The rest of the presents were given to these men. Through signs, the French indicated that they were leaving for the night, but that they very much wished to see the islanders again on the morrow, in order to give them more presents. The natives in turn indicated that they slept nearby and that they would return punctually.

"In general," said La Pérouse, "we believed that they were the owners of a storage shed for fish, which we had come upon at the side of the stream and which is raised on stakes four or five feet above the ground. When he visited this place, M. de Langle respected it as he had the abandoned cabins; he found that it contained salmon, dried and smoked herring, bladders filled with oil, and parchment-thin salmon skins.

"This warehouse is too large for the sustenance of one family, and he decided that the people are engaged in trading these various products."

The next day La Pérouse himself went ashore. The islanders, followed by another canoe, arrived promptly in the cove. In all there were twenty-one men and no women. The dogs barking in the woods indicated that they had been left there with the women. The French wanted to enter the forest, but the islanders very energetically sought to divert them from their purpose. Wishing to win their confidence, La Pérouse ordered his men to give up their scheme. Various presents were given to the natives, who seem to value only useful articles, especially iron and textile fabrics. They prefer silver to copper, copper to iron, thus revealing their knowledge of metals. They are very poor; only three or four have silver earrings decorated with blue glass, similar to those found at Ternei Bay and taken

Dress of natives at De Langle Bay

for bracelets. Their other little ornaments are of copper. Their pipes and tinderboxes seem to be Chinese or Japanese, the former being very skillfully made of an alloy of copper and zinc. By pointing to the west, they made it clear that the blue nankeen which some of them were wearing, the glassware, and the tinderboxes came from the country of the Manchu, a word which they pronounce exactly as the French do.

"When they saw that we all had paper and pencil at hand in order to compile a vocabulary of their language, they guessed our plan. They anticipated our questions, brought us various objects, supplied the name of the country, and were obliging enough to repeat words four or five times, until they were sure that we had correctly learned their pronunciation. The ease with which they had guessed our intentions led me to believe that the art of writing was not unknown to them. They seemed very eager for our hatchets and cloth; they did not even fear to ask for them, but they were careful not to take anything which had not been given to them. Evidently they have the same concept of stealing as we have, and I would not have feared to entrust them with the care of our goods. In this connection, they scrupulously avoided taking even one of the salmon we had caught, even though the fish were spread by the thousands on the beach, for our catch had been as plentiful as on the day before. We had repeatedly to urge them to take as much as they wanted.

"When in the course of the conversation they discovered that we wanted them to make a sketch of their country and of Manchuria, a very old man rose, and with the end of his pipe he drew the coast of Tartary to the west, running nearly north to south; to the east and in the same direction, he sketched his island and, by placing his hand on his chest, indicated that he had just drawn his own country. Between Tartary and his island he left a strait, and, turning toward the frigates, he showed by a stroke that they could pass through it. To the south of this island he had drawn another island and had left a strait, showing that this was also a route for the ships. Another islander, seeing that the drawings in the sand were being obliterated, took one of our pencils and some paper. On this he drew his island, which he named Choka [Sakhalin Island], and with a stroke he indicated the stream at which we were, placing it about two-thirds the length of the island from north to south. He then sketched

Manchuria, leaving, as did the old man, a strait at the end of the funnel and adding, to our great surprise, the Segalien River, whose name the islanders pronounce as we do. He placed the mouth of this river a little to the south of the point of his island, and with seven strokes he showed the number of days by canoe necessary for the trip from where we were to the mouth of the Segalien. By some strokes, he also showed how many days by canoe it takes to ascend the river to where they obtain the blue nankeen and other trade goods through their transactions with the people living in these regions. As the other islanders witnessed this conversation, their gestures confirmed their compatriot's statements. Finally by his signs, he clearly showed how wide the river and the strait are, but it was impossible to guess what he tried to make us understand regarding the depth of the water. The bay was named De Langle Bay [Tomari]."

The remainder of the day was used in exploring the country. The French were very surprised to find that a people who live by hunting and fishing, cultivating none of the products of nature and with no herds of domesticated animals, should have, for the most part, gentle, sober habits and perhaps a higher intelligence than the common people of Europe. The fabrics which were given to them they turned in every direction, discussing them with each other and seeking to determine how they had been manufactured. They are acquainted with the shuttle. La Pérouse bought a loom with which they make cloth exactly like the French product, except that the thread is made of the bark of a willow tree very common on the island. They are very skilled in exploiting the natural products of the land. Their cabins contain a large quantity of the roots of a species of yellow lily or the Kamchatka *saranne*, which they dry; this provides them with food during the winter. There is also plenty of garlic and angelica; these plants grow on the edge of the forests.

For the most part well formed, these islanders have strong constitutions and pleasant faces, and dress in an unusual manner. They are small in stature, none of those seen being over five feet five inches, and several being less than five feet tall. They allowed the artists from the frigates to sketch them but firmly opposed efforts of the surgeon to measure the various parts of their bodies. Perhaps they believed that he was a magician. On his thumb, each wears a heavy ring shaped like a doughnut; these

Niskani, Aoucantouri and Erougantoi, natives of De Langle Bay

Oroches, *natives of De Castries Bay*

rings are made of ivory, horn, or lead. They have the same customs as the Chinese, as, for example, in greeting each other and in allowing their nails to grow long. The Chinese sailors who were on board the French frigates did not understand a single word of the islanders' language, but they easily understood the two Manchurian Tartars who had crossed over from the continent about twenty days ago, perhaps to purchase fish.

"We met with them only in the afternoon. They carried on a lively conversation with one of our Chinese. They gave him exactly the same geographical description of the country, changing only the place names, evidently because these are different in each language. The Tartars' clothing is made of grey nankeen, like that of the coolies or porters of Macao, and they wear pointed hats made of bark. In manners and appearance they are much less pleasing than the islanders. They said they lived eight days' journey up the Segalien River.

"The islanders' cabins are skillfully constructed; every precaution is taken against the cold. They are built of wood covered with birch bark, the roof consisting of a framework overlaid with thatch; there is a very low door in a gabled entrance; the fireplace is in the center, under an opening in the roof through which the smoke leaves. Little board benches, eight to ten inches high, circle the interior, the floor of which is covered with mats. The cabin just described is located in the middle of a grove of rose bushes, one hundred paces from the seashore. The shrubs were blossoming and gave off a delightful fragrance, but not enough to overcome the stench of fish and oil which would have prevailed against all the perfumes of Arabia. The natives are never without their pipes, smoking a good quality, long-leafed tobacco which, I believe, they import from Tartary. But they made it clear to us that their pipes come from the island to the south, obviously Japan.

"At dawn the following day, the frigates departed and tacked in the midst of fogs until the 19th. On that day, still on the same coast, they dropped anchor in a bay which was named D'Estaing Bay.[3] Our boats

---

[3] Henri Comte d'Estaing (1729–1794), a French admiral, was born at the Chateau of Ravel, Auvergne. He became famous fighting the English in Asian and American waters. After testifying in favor of Marie Antoinette in 1793, he was tried and executed in 1794.

landed there, below ten or twelve cabins located haphazardly at a considerable distance from each other and about a hundred paces from the edge of the sea. They are a little larger than those already described. They are constructed of the same materials but are divided into two rooms. The inner room contains all the small household furniture, the fireplace, and the circular bench. The vestibule, however, is completely empty and seems intended for receiving visitors, since strangers probably are not permitted to see the women. Some officers, however, found two who had fled and were hiding in the grass. When our boats landed in the cove, some frightened women shrieked as if they were about to be devoured; however, they were in the care of an islander who brought them to their homes and seemed to be trying to calm them. They are fairly good-looking, although a little unusual; their eyes are small, their lips large, the upper one being tattooed or painted blue. Their legs are bare, and their attire consists of a long dressing gown. They wear their hair long and do not follow the male practice of shaving the crown of the head.

"M. de Langle, who was the first ashore, found the islanders gathered around four canoes loaded with fish; they were helping to launch the canoes, and he learned that the twenty-four men who made up the crews were Manchurians who had come from the banks of the Segalien River to buy this fish. He had a long conversation with them through our Chinese, whom they welcomed most cordially. They confirmed all the geographical data which we had received earlier. In one out-of-the-way spot, M. de Langle also came across a kind of circle formed by fifteen to twenty stakes, each of which was topped by a bear head. The bones of these animals were scattered about nearby. Since these people have no firearms, since they fight the bears hand to hand, and since their arrows can only wound the beasts, we believed that this circle was intended to commemorate their victories and that the twenty exposed bear heads were the trophies of the past decade, judging by the state of decomposition which most of them had reached. The character of the soil and its products at D'Estaing Bay is practically the same as at De Langle Bay; the salmon is as abundant, and each cabin has its storage shed. We learned that these people eat the head, the tail, and the backbone; the salmon fillets they smoke and dry, to be sold to the Manchurians. For themselves they keep only the smoke, which permeates their homes, their furniture, their clothing, and even the grass which grows around their villages. After heaping presents upon the Tartars and the islanders, we departed in our boats.

"As we advanced northward, the coast of Choka became much steeper and more mountainous than along the southern part. We saw neither fire nor dwelling. For the first time since we left the coast of Tartary, we caught eight or ten codfish, an indication that we were near the mainland which we had lost sight of after passing 47° latitude.

"Forced to follow one coast or the other, I preferred that of the island, in order not to miss the strait, if there was one leading to the east, a task which required the greatest care because of the fogs which left us only the briefest intervals of clear weather. I was boxed in, as it were, and was never more than two leagues from shore between De Langle Bay and the end of the channel. My guesses regarding the proximity of the Tartary coast were so well founded that as soon as visibility increased we had a perfect view of it. At 50° latitude, the channel begins to narrow and is no more than twelve or thirteen leagues wide.

"Since I had seen no dwelling after leaving D'Estaing Bay, I sent M. de Clonard with four boats to investigate a cove into which flows a small stream. Three leagues from the stream is an unusual peak, which was named La Martinière Peak. M. de Clonard returned at eight o'clock in the evening and, to my surprise, all his boats were full of salmon, although the crews had neither nets nor lines. He had landed at the mouth of a stream which is about twenty-five feet wide and about one foot deep. He had found it so filled with salmon that the bed was completely covered with them, and our sailors, using sticks, killed five thousand two hundred fish in an hour. Otherwise, they discovered only two or three abandoned shelters believed to have been put up by Manchurians who were accustomed to come from the mainland to trade in the southern part of this island. The vegetation is much hardier than at the bays where the previous landings had been made; the trees are considerably larger; celery and watercress grow in abundance on the banks of this stream. They could also have gathered enough juniper berries to fill several sacks. The pines and the willows are much more numerous than the oak, maple, birch, and hawthorn trees, and if other travelers coming after us land on the banks of this stream, they will pick quantities of currants, strawberries, and raspberries, which were still in blossom. There was nothing to indicate that the country has any metal.

"On July 25, at 50° 54′ north latitude, we raised a very fine bay, the only one in our voyage along this island which provides ships a secure shelter against the north winds. Here and there on the shore are some dwellings near a ravine which marks the bed of a stream somewhat larger than those which we had already seen. I was in such a hurry and the clear weather which we were enjoying was so valuable for us that I thought I ought to use it to make more northing. I wanted to find out whether this strait, which the islanders and the Manchurians had mentioned to me, could be used. I began to fear that it was not navigable, because the depth decreased very rapidly as we progressed northward and because the terrain of the island now consisted of dunes and swamps almost at the level of the sea, like sand banks.

"Indeed the sequence of events convinced us that the bottom of the channel slopes upward from south to north, somewhat like a river which becomes shallower as one approaches its source. The depth decreases rapidly at the rate of three fathoms a league. Assuming a uniform slope, I calculated that at this rate scarcely six leagues remained before we reached the end of the gulf. In the course of time, the entire channel ends at a bar, still hidden by shallow water, which completely closes the strait, leaving no waterway or thoroughfare of any kind. Someday no doubt, as it rises, this bank will join the island with the Tartary mainland.

"At evening on July 28, we reached this Tartary coast where it forms an opening which was named De Castries Bay.[4] It provides a safe anchorage, and the two frigates dropped anchor there. There is a very large

---

[4] Marquis Charles de Castries (1727–1801), Marshal of France, was born at Castries, Herault. He was Minister of the Navy from 1780 to 1787 and became an émigré in 1791.

inlet beside which is a village. At first, we believed it deep enough to take our ships because the tide was in when we anchored in the middle of the bay. Two hours later it had become a vast field of wrack and weed, leaping with salmon which were coming out of a stream lost among the water plants. There, in one day, we caught more than two thousand of these fish.

"The natives, whose livelihood is assured by the very plentiful supply of salmon, were not troubled when they saw how successful we were, no doubt because they were certain that the supply was inexhaustible. We landed at the foot of their village.

"You could not meet a finer group of people. The chief, or eldest, accompanied by several other men, came to receive us on the beach. He greeted us in the Chinese manner, by performing the kowtow, and then led us into his cabin where we saw his wife, his daughters-in-law, his children, and his grandchildren. He had a fresh mat rolled out for us to sit upon. We were given some salmon and a small-grained cereal cooked in a kettle; we did not recognize the grain, which is their most important food. They indicated that the grain came from the country of the Manchu and that they themselves were *Oroches*. Pointing out four canoes which we had seen entering the bay the same day and which had stopped at the village, they described the visiting crews as *Bitchys*, who live seven or eight leagues to the south. As do the natives of Canada, these people change their language and nationality from one village to another.

"The Orochene village consists of four cabins, solidly built of full-length fir logs neatly cut at the corners. A well-constructed framework supports the roof, which is made of bark. Inside they resemble the cabins on Choka Island. We had reason to believe that these four dwellings belong to four different families who live in perfect harmony. We saw one of these families leave on a long trip, since they did not return during the five days which we spent in this bay. The owners placed some boards in front of the door of their home to keep out the dogs and left all their belongings there. Before long, we were so convinced of the absolute honesty of these people and their almost religious respect for private property that, trusting their integrity, we left our packs in the middle of their cabins, even though the packs were filled with cloth, beads, iron tools, and other trade goods. The natives never abused our complete confidence in them.

Dress of natives at De Castries Bay

"Each cabin is surrounded with salmon-drying equipment. The fish, after having been smoked for three or four days around the fireplace, which is in the middle of the cabin, are hung on poles and exposed to the heat of the sun. The women responsible for this work have to allow the smoke to permeate the fish before taking them out of doors where they become as hard as boards.

"They caught their fish in the same stream as we did, using nets or spears; it sickened us to watch them greedily eating the raw snouts, gills, bones, and sometimes the entire skin, which they remove from the salmon with great dexterity. They suck the viscous liquid of these parts as we swallow an oyster. Most of the fish are skinned before they are brought to the cabins, except when the catch has been very plentiful. Then the women just as eagerly search for the whole salmon and are equally disgusting in the way they devour the mucilaginous parts, which they seem to consider the most delicious delicacy. Here at De Castries Bay we learned the purpose of the lead or bone rings which these people and those of Choka Island wear on their thumbs; it gives them leverage when they cut and skin the salmon with the sharp knife which each of them wears hanging from his belt.

"Their village is built upon a low, marshy tongue of land with a southern exposure, which to us seemed uninhabitable during the winter. On the opposite side of the bay, however, on higher ground, facing south and at the entrance to a forest, there is a second village, consisting of eight cabins which are much larger and better built than the first ones. Above it and a short distance beyond, we examined three underground dwellings, exactly like those of the natives of Kamchatka described in Cook's last voyage. They are large enough to accommodate the tenants of the eight cabins during the coldest part of the winter and are completely furnished, even though they remain deserted as long as the weather is pleasant.

"Finally, at one end of this little village, we found several tombs which were better built and just as large as the cabins; each contained three, four, or five neatly fashioned coffins. The coffins were covered with Chinese fabrics, some of which were brocade. Bows, arrows, nets, and in general the most valuable possessions of these people are hung up inside these sepulchral structures, which have wooden doors locked by a crossbar held in place by two brackets. The bodies of the poor are placed out of doors, in a coffin set upon a round platform supported by stakes four feet high. Each one has his bow and arrows, his net, and some pieces of cloth on his monument; to remove any of these articles would probably be a sacrilege.

"It was evident that we had visited only the *Oroches*' country homes, where they catch the salmon which, like wheat in Europe, is the mainstay of their subsistence. I saw so little elkhide there that I was forced to conclude that they do very little hunting. Likewise, it is my opinion that the roots of the Kamchatka lily, which the women dig up along the edges of the woods and which they dry by their fireplaces, form only a very small part of their diet.

"Undoubtedly the various families who comprise this tribe are scattered among the neighboring bays where they catch and dry salmon. They come together only in the winter, bringing with them their supplies of fish on which they live until the warm weather returns. This explains why we saw so few natives.

"These people, as well as the Choka Islanders, do not seem to recognize the authority of any leader or government. The gentleness of their manners and their respect for old people minimize the disadvantages of their anarchy. We never witnessed the slightest quarrel. Their mutual affection and their fondness for their children were touching to behold. On the other hand, our stomachs were turned by the foul smell of salmon which pervades their homes and the surrounding area. Around the hearths are scattered fish bones and blood, refuse eaten by dogs which are quite gentle and friendly despite their hunger. These people are revoltingly malodorous and squalid. No other people are so meager and so ill-favored. Their average height is less than four feet ten inches, they are thin, and their voices are as weak and shrill as children's. They have prominent cheekbones, small, slanted, bleary eyes, a large mouth, a flat nose, a short, almost beardless chin, and an olive skin impregnated with oil and smoke. The men do not cut their hair but tie it in braids; the women let theirs fall loose upon their shoulders. There is only a slight difference between men's clothing and that of the women. The latter are not subjected to any kind of forced labor; their only tasks are to make clothes, dry fish, and care for their children, whom they nurse for three or four years.

"The women seem to enjoy a considerable amount of respect. No bargain is closed without their approval, and the silver earrings and the copper jewelry worn on clothing are reserved exclusively for women and girls. The men and boys wear tunics made of nankeen or of dog or fish skin cut like a teamster's smock. If it extends below the knees, they do not wear drawers; otherwise, they wear them down to the calf, as the Chinese do. Everybody has sealskin boots, but they are kept for the winter. People of all ages, even children still at the breast, always wear a leather belt to which are attached a sheath-knife, a tinderbox, a tobacco pouch, and a pipe.

"The women wear loose fitting gowns made of nankeen or of salmon skin which they are able to make very soft through expert tanning. This garment reaches down to their ankles; sometimes it is fringed with little copper ornaments which make a tinkling sound. The salmon which provide the skins for these robes weigh thirty to forty pounds and are not caught in the summer. The ones which we had just caught in July weighed only three or four pounds, but their number and excellent flavor made up for their size. All of us agreed that we had never tasted better salmon.

"We can say nothing of this tribe's religion, since we saw no shrine and no priests but only some crudely carved figures which may have been idols; hanging from the ceiling of their cabins, these represent children, arms, legs, hands . . . Perhaps these images which we took for idols are only mementoes of a child killed by a bear or some hunter wounded by these beasts; yet it is hardly likely that such underdeveloped people should be free of superstition. Sometimes we suspected that they took us for magicians. Although they answered politely, our questions always worried them, and when we drew diagrams on paper, they seemed to think that the motions of the hand in writing were magical signs."

The travelers whose four canoes had been beached in front of the village aroused the curiosity of the French. When they were questioned about the geography of the entire region, their answers confirmed all the conjectures which La Pérouse had made regarding the sand bank which blocks the northern end of the gulf. Furthermore, the two officers who had been sent ahead to make soundings reported that the water was rapidly becoming very shallow. It was late in the season, and La Pérouse was under no illusions regarding the difficulty of navigating a narrow channel enveloped in fog. Consequently, on the morning of August 2, the frigates set sail and after raising the Tartary coast they steered toward Choka, the coast of which they followed until they reached its southern end, which they named Cape Krilon. To the south lay the island of Hokkaido.

It was at Cape Krilon that the French were first visited by the Choka Islanders, who were somewhat defiant and unapproachable until the French spoke some words of the vocabulary compiled at De Langle Bay by the surgeon of the *Astrolabe*. Soon they felt completely secure; they sat in a circle on the quarterdeck, and there they smoked their pipes. They were loaded with gifts—nankeen, silk, hardware, beads, tobacco, and in general whatever the French thought would please them. It was soon noted that brandy and tobacco are what they prize most. These, however, were the very goods which La Pérouse distributed most sparingly, "because," as he said, "the crew needed the tobacco, and I feared the consequences of the brandy."

These men have as strong physiques and as much body-hair as the natives at De Langle Bay. They are as swarthy as Algerians and the other peoples of the Barbary Coast. Their behavior is dignified, and courtly are the gestures by which they express their thanks. They became annoying, however, by the persistence of their entreaties for more presents. Moreover, their gratitude never prompted them to offer the French even some of the salmon which filled their canoes; they put part of their salmon ashore because they did not receive the excessively high price which they asked for it. What a difference in moral qualities between these people and the *Oroches*, whom they so surpass in strength and skill!

The French never saw these islanders dance nor did they ever hear them sing, but they noticed that all of them are able to produce music of a sort with the main stem of a large celery plant or a species of spurge. The pipe is open on both ends, and they blow on the small end to make sounds very like those of a muted trumpet. This is apparently the only musical instrument which they have.

These islanders weave all of their own clothing. Their homes are so clean and attractive that they cannot be compared with those on the mainland, and they have artistic furniture, almost all of which is made in Japan. The mainstay of their economy is whale oil, which is unknown in Manchuria; all of their wealth is earned by trading this commodity. They produce a great amount of it, although their method of extracting the oil is not the most efficient. They cut up the flesh of the whale, and placing it on an inclined surface exposed to the sun they let it decompose in the open air; the oil which flows down is collected in bark containers or sealskin bottles. It is very remarkable that the French did not see a single whale off the west coast of the island, although they are plentiful on the eastern side.

The islanders who had come aboard the frigates left before nightfall, indicating by signs that they would return the next day. They arrived exactly at daybreak, bringing with them some salmon which they traded for hatchets and knives. They also sold a sword and a cloth coat of local manufacture. They seemed disappointed when they saw the French preparing to leave and entreated them to round Cape Krilon and stop in a cove which they described and called *Tabuero*. This was Cape Aniva.

Among these islanders there seems to exist a distinction in social standing which is not present among the natives of the Tartary coast. Each canoe has one man with whom the others do not associate; he does not eat with them and seems to be absolutely subject to them. He may be a slave, but in any case his rank is very inferior to that of the others.

A boat was sent to shore with orders to return before midnight. The officer who commanded the party and his companions had been cordially welcomed in the village at Cape Krilon. He did some trading and brought back a large amount of salmon. He found the houses better built and especially more richly decorated than those at D'Estaing Bay; in several of them, the furnishings include large lacquered vases from Japan. The French climbed to the highest point on the cape, from where they were able to take the bearings of various landmarks and to observe that a strait separates Choka from Hokkaido.

On August 10, La Pérouse left Krilon Bay. Tossed about during the entire night by a powerful swell in the midst of a dead calm, which placed them in the greatest danger of running afoul of each other, the frigates found themselves north of the village of Chica, referred to as Acqueis in the report of the voyage of the Dutch vessel *Kastrikum*. "We had just crossed," said La Pérouse, "a strait twelve leagues wide separating Hokkaido from Choka. No European vessel had ever made the crossing before. This passage had escaped the notice of other navigators. The Dutch on the *Kastrikum*, crossing from Acqueis to Aniva, passed in front of this strait without suspecting its presence because of the fogs and without realizing, when they had anchored at Aniva, that they were on another island, so similar are these people in appearance, customs, and manners."

The next day the weather was excellent and the frigates went out of the channel, which was appropriately named La Pérouse Strait. On the 20th, they sighted Urup and, despite the heavy overcast, recognized De Vries Strait. Finally, on August 30, they cut across the Kuril Islands chain through a strait which La Pérouse named Boussole Channel, between Simushir and Chirpoi. He wanted to make a detailed reconnaissance of the northern islands of the archipelago, but the fogs were so continuous and so heavy that he was forced to give up his plan and instead to steer a course for Kamchatka.

CHAPTER VIII

Anchorage in Avatcha Bay
The Kindness of the Governor of Kamchatka
  toward the Crews of the Frigates
News from France
Departure of Lesseps the Interpreter
The Expedition Leaves Avatcha Bay

UNTIL SEPTEMBER 5 the fog was even more persistent than it had previously been, but since they were on the open sea, they crowded sail in the midst of the darkness, and at six o'clock in the evening the weather cleared enough to make the Kamchatka coast visible. On September 6, they recognized Avatcha or Petropavlovsk Bay, which they entered on the 7th. The governor came out five leagues in his canoe to meet the French and to inform them that they had been expected for a long time. They had scarcely dropped anchor when they saw the pastor of Paratunka come on board. A moment later they were welcomed by the headman and several other residents of the village, each bringing a gift of salmon and skate. Lieutenant Aborov, commander of Petropavlovsk harbor, overwhelmed the newcomers with courtesy and placed at their disposal his home, his soldiers, and everything they needed.

The astonomers had hardly set up their observatory when the naturalists, who were no less zealous, decided that they would inspect the volcano, although this involved a trip of several leagues and a climb to the summit where the crater was located.

The mouth of this crater, turned toward Avatcha Bay, provided the French with the spectacle of continuous eddies of smoke. At one time during the night, they saw blue and yellow flames which rose only a short distance. Determined to overcome all obstacles, the naturalists started off, accompanied by Cossacks who carried their equipment, which consisted of a tent, fur clothing, and provisions for four days. They themselves carried their delicate scientific instruments. The first stop was in the woods. They had little difficulty in moving across the terrain, which was covered with plants and trees, mostly birches. At sunset, they pitched their tent, built a fire, and made all arrangements for the night. The next day at dawn, the trip was resumed. There had been a heavy snowfall during the night and, what was even worse, a dense fog covered the peak of the volcano, the base of which the travelers did not reach until three o'clock in the afternoon. Their guides stopped as soon as they reached the timber line. They pitched their tents and lit their fires. This night's rest was essential before undertaking the ascent on the next day. At six o'clock in the morning they began to climb, and they did not stop until they had reached the lower part of the crater's edge at three o'clock in the afternoon. They often had to use their hands in order to avoid falling down the jagged, rocky walls of the frightful chasms which they passed.

This mountain consists entirely of lava which is more or less porous and could almost be classified as pumice; gypseous material and sulphurous crystallization are found on the summit. The schorls and all the other stones are not as beautiful as those of the volcano at Tenerife. Nevertheless, the naturalists brought back several fine specimens of chrysolite. The weather was so bad and so much snow had fallen that they were forced to return much sooner than they had planned.

M. Kaslov, the governor-general of the peninsula, finally arrived at Petropavlovsk. A man of utmost refinement and most courteous manners, he spoke French and had a wide range of knowledge, especially in geography and natural history. The French wondered how an officer who would have been distinguished among the most cultured people could have been banished to the end of the earth, to a nation which was completely uncivilized. The following day, he invited his guests to a ball which he wished to give in their honor for all the women, the Kamchatkan as well as the Russian. Although the gathering was not large, it was at least unusual. Thirteen women, dressed in silk, were seated on benches around the parlor. Ten of these were Kamchatkans with broad faces, small eyes, and flat noses. Each wore a silk kerchief about her head, in the style of the mulatto women in our colonies. They began with some Russian dances accompanied by very pleasant music which greatly resembled that of the Cossacks. Next came the Kamchatkan dances, in which only the arms and shoulders are used while the legs remain almost motionless. The convolutions and contortions of the dancers filled the spectators with dismay, and this feeling was made even more acute by the dancers' guttural cries of anguish, which served as their musical accompaniment. So violent was the dance that the women were dripping with sweat and fell exhausted, unable to rise. The fumes emanating from their bodies filled the apartment with an odor of fish oil to which European sensitivities were completely unadapted. La Pérouse asked the meaning of the wild dance which two of the women had just finished. He was told that they had just enacted a bear hunt. As a reward for the show which they had performed, each of the dancers received a glass of brandy.

No sooner was the dancing ended when a cheery shout announced the arrival of a messenger from Okhotsk, with letters from Europe for La Pérouse. The news made everyone happy, but most of all the expedition's commander, who had been promoted to the rank of rear admiral.

The governor-general wanted to celebrate this event by discharging all the cannon in the place, and he overwhelmed La Pérouse with acts of friendship and affection. He gave the officers of the frigates all kinds of presents, which his affableness forced them to accept. In recognition of his kindness, they gave him a copy of the *Report of Cook's Third Voyage*, which seemed to please him immensely. He was acquainted with all the persons mentioned in the report. As M. Shemalev, the good pastor of Paratunka, and the unfortunate Ivashklin[1] heard the governor translate

---

[1] La Pérouse took a keen interest in finding the aged Ivashklin in Kamchatka, since the English newspapers had entertained Europe for a long time with reports of him. This interest increased when he learned that this poor chap's only crime consisted of some indiscreet remarks concerning Empress Elizabeth made as he was leaving a supper party where the wine had muddled his mind. He was less than twenty years old at the time. An officer of the guards, a member of a distinguished Russian family, and a sociable character, he was drummed out and banished to the end of Kamchatka, after having been flogged and having his nostrils slit. Empress Catherine had pardoned him

the passages which concerned them, they exclaimed that Cook was absolutely correct.

The French made a survey of Avatcha Bay. Without fear of contradiction, this bay is one of the loveliest, safest, and most convenient that can be found anywhere. Two huge harbors, one on the eastern and one on the western shore, can accommodate all of the ships of the French and English navies. The village of Petropavlovsk is located on a tongue of land which, like a pier, forms a small enclosed area behind the village. Three or four unarmed vessels could spend the winter in this circular enclosure. The entrance of this basin is less than one hundred fifty feet wide; nature could not have been more accommodating.

"It is not at all to foreign navigators," said La Pérouse, "that Russia is obliged for her discoveries and outposts on the shores of eastern Tartary and on the Kamchatka peninsula. The Russians, who sought furs as eagerly as the Spanish searched for gold and silver, have long been making arduous and distant explorations by land in order to obtain the valuable skins of the sable, fox, and sea otter. More soldiers than hunters, however, they found it more convenient to conquer the natives and to make them pay tribute than to share with them the fatigue of hunting. They did not discover the peninsula of Kamchatka until the end of the seventeenth century; their first camgaign against the liberty of the unfortunate natives took place in 1696. Russian authority was not fully established throughout the peninsula until 1711.

"A complete account of the value of Russia's colonies in the Far East must indicate that the land explorations were followed by voyages east of

---

several years ago, but living more than fifty years in the forests of Kamchatka, in addition to the memory and the shame of an unjust punishment, made him ignore this act of justice, and he persisted in his resolve to die in Siberia. La Pérouse sympathetically begged him to accept some tobacco, powder, lead, cloth, and whatever else he thought could be useful for him. Ivashklin had been raised in Paris, still understood a little French, and recalled more than enough words to express his gratitude. At the same time, he did the travelers a service by showing them the tomb of Delisle de la Croyère, astronomer and geographer, who died in 1741 upon the return of an expedition commissioned by the czar to explore the coast of America. The French consecrated the memory of their fellow countryman by placing an inscription upon his tombstone and by giving his name to an island near the places he had visited.—Valentin

View of St. Peter and St. Paul, Kamchatka

Kamchatka toward the shores of America, those of Bering and Chirikof being known throughout Europe. After the names of these men, made famous by their expeditions and the hardships involved, we can list other navigators who added to the Russian Empire the Aleutian Islands, a group farther to the east known as the Unalaska Islands, and all the islands south of the Kamchatka peninsula.

"Russia spent very little money to acquire these possessions. Merchants sent equipment to Okhotsk, where, at great expense, they built ships forty-five to fifty feet long, with only one mast in the middle, somewhat like our cutters, and carrying forty to fifty men who were all hunters rather than sailors. Those who left Okhotsk in the month of June usually went out between Cape Lopatka and the first of the Kuril Islands, sailed eastward, and visited various islands for three or four years until they had either bought from the natives or themselves killed a sufficiently great number of otters to cover the costs of the undertaking and to give the investors a profit of at least one hundred percent.

"On their way back, these vessels sometimes stopped at Avatcha Bay, but they always returned to Okhotsk, which was the residence of the owners or the merchants who traded directly with the Chinese over the frontier of the two empires. Since Avatcha Bay is never closed by ice, the Russian navigators stopped there when it was too late in the season to reach Okhotsk before the end of September. A wise rule has prohibited navigation in the Sea of Okhotsk after this date which marks the beginning of the hurricanes and squalls which have caused many shipwrecks on this sea.

"In Avatcha Bay, the ice never extends more than seven or eight yards from the shore. During the winter, it often happens that the off-shore winds dislodge some of the ice blocking the mouths of the Paratunka and Avatcha Rivers, which then become navigable. Since the winter is generally less rigorous in Kamchatka than in St. Petersburg and various Russian provinces, the Russians speak of it as the French speak of the winters of Provence. However, the snowfall which we experienced on September 20 and the frost which covered the ground every morning made us believe that the cold would be so severe that southern Europeans could not stand it.

"We were, however, in certain respects less chilly than the Russian or Kamchatkan residents of the Petropavlovsk ostrog, or district. They are clad in the thickest furs, and the temperature inside their log houses, where they always have a fire in the stoves, is from 28° to 30° above freezing.[2] We could not breathe in such hot air, and the governor was careful to open his windows when we were in his apartment. These people are accustomed to extremes, and it is well known that in Europe as well as in Asia people are in the habit of taking steam baths in furnace rooms from which they come covered with sweat and then immediately go and roll in the snow.

"The Petropavlovsk ostrog has two of these public baths, which I entered before the stoves were lighted. They consist of a very low room in the center of which is a stone oven, heated like a baking oven. For the bathers, there are tiers of benches encircling the vaulted oven, so that the higher ones receive more heat, the lower less. When the top of the vault is red hot from the fire within, water is thrown on it. This water immediately rises in the form of steam and causes the bathers to perspire most profusely.

"The Kamchatkans have adopted this as well as many other customs of their rulers. At present their population numbers not over four thousand persons in the entire peninsula, which extends from 51° to 63° and is several degrees of longitude wide. Thus, it is evident that there are several square leagues of land for each member of the population. They do not cultivate the earth, and their preference for dogs instead of reindeer for hauling sleds prevents them from raising pigs, sheep, young reindeer, colts, and calves, because these animals would be eaten before they became strong enough to defend themselves. Fish is the main food of the dog-teams, which can make up to twenty-four leagues a day; they are not fed until they have completed their day's journey. This method of traveling is not peculiar to the Kamchatkan people, as dog-teams are the only method used in Choka and by the Tartars at De Castries Bay.

"We were very anxious to know if the Russians were acquainted with

---

[2] Assuming that La Pérouse was using the Réaumur scale, this was a Fahrenheit equivalent of about 97°.

these different countries, and we learned from M. Kaslov that the ships from Okhotsk had occasionally sighted the northern point of the island which is opposite the mouth of the Amur River, but they had never sailed farther because it is beyond the limits of the settlements of the Russian Empire on this coast."

The pastor of Paratunka gave the officers of the expedition detailed information about the Kurils, which are under his spiritual direction and which he visits each year. The Russians have found it more convenient to substitute numbers for the traditional names of these islands, thus, they speak of the first, the second, etc., until they reach the twenty-first, where their claims end. Only four of the twenty-one islands are inhabited, the first, the second, the thirteenth, and the fourteenth; the others are absolutely deserted, with the islanders landing there only to hunt otter and fox. Several of the uninhabited islands are no more than islets or large rocks, and there is no wood on any of them. The total population of the four inhabited islands amounts to no more than fourteen hundred persons. They have very hairy bodies, wear long beards, and make their livelihood by sealing, fishing, and hunting. Moreover, they are good, hospitable, tractable people, all of whom have adopted the Christian religion.

Governor-General Kaslov proved so obliging to his guests that La Pérouse had only to ask in order to receive permission to send his journal to France with Lesseps,[3] a young man who had shipped with him as his Russian interpreter. At the same time, he believed he could render his country a service by providing an energetic young man with the opportunity to make his own observation of the various provinces of the vast Russian Empire. In addition, M. Kaslov declared that he would take him as his aide-de-camp until they reached Okhotsk, where he would help him make arrangements for the trip to St. Petersburg. At the moment of their departure, the officers of the frigates, as if they secretly anticipated the tragic fate which awaited them, were unable to suppress their feeling of tenderness. There were tears in their eyes as they left a friend whose fine qualities had endeared him to them and who was about to travel through

---

[3] Barthelemy de Lesseps (1766–1834) was the son of the French Consul-General in St. Petersburg.

a strange country on a journey which was as dangerous as it was long.[4]

The cold now warned La Pérouse that it was time to think about leaving. The country, which at his arrival on September 7 he had found so beautifully green, was as yellow and sere on September 25 as it is at the end of December in the vicinity of Paris. Snow covered all the mountains at elevations greater than twelve hundred feet above sea level. The commander, therefore, issued orders to prepare everything for departure, and on the 29th they set sail. M. Kaslov came to bid farewell to the crews, and since the calm forced the frigates to anchor in the middle of the bay, he had dinner on board. La Pérouse, together with Captain de Langle and several officers, accompanied him ashore where he gave them an excellent supper and another ball. They finally parted, but not without some emotion. The next day at dawn, the wind having changed to the north, the signal to get under way appeared, and soon the French saw the last of this land of fond memory, where they had received the most considerate and attentive hospitality.

The north winds, which favored the departure of the frigates from Avatcha Bay, died down about ten leagues out to sea, and the west winds set in so violently and unyieldingly that La Pérouse was frequently obliged to have the trysail rigged on the foremast. He then steered a course to 165° longitude and 37° 30′ latitude, where some geographers have placed a large island supposedly discovered by the Spanish in 1620. On October 14, they saw some small land birds, a species of linnet, which perched on the ship's rigging, flights of ducks, and some cormorants. These birds never wander far from shore. The weather was very clear and lookouts were constantly at the mast tops on both ships. A substantial

---

[4] Lesseps left Petropavlovsk on October 7, 1787. The journey to St. Petersburg was filled with countless adventures and dangers which are vividly described in his diary. The young interpreter allowed nothing to stand in his way and accomplished his mission most conscientiously by reporting the results of the expedition's efforts in France. He was the only one of the French crew who was destined to return to his native land. Readers who wish more detailed information of Kamchatka can consult the historic journal of Lesseps' trip, published in Paris in 1790. The details found there are certainly the most accurate and the most interesting ever published on that region. —Valentin

reward was promised the first man to sight land, but competition among the sailors was increased by a much more powerful motive. If land were found, it would be named after the first man to point it out.

The search was fruitless. While it was going on, a tragic accident occurred. A sailor on board the *Astrolabe* fell into the sea while he was furling the fore topgallant sail. Whether he was killed by the fall or could not swim, the poor fellow never reappeared, and all the efforts of his comrades to save him were in vain.

CHAPTER IX

The Samoan Islands—Anchorage at Mauna
Massacre of Captain de Langle
*   and Eleven Members of the Two Crews*
Observation of Oiolava and Pola Islands

AFTER THE MANY EFFORTS which the search for the island of the Spaniards required of the crews, La Pérouse decided to sail into the southern hemisphere, into that vast expanse where Quiros, Mendana, Tasman, and Cook made their voyages of discovery, along routes which since have been crossed in every direction by modern navigators, into that equatorial ocean which contains an area extending 12° to 15° from north to south and 140° from east to west, where islands are as lavishly sprinkled upon our planet as the stars in the Milky Way. It was into this region of islands that his instructions ordered him to sail during the third year of his voyage.

The winds were changing and the sea rough until the expedition reached 30° latitude, on October 29. They soon were enjoying clear skies, and on November 5 they intersected the line which they had followed on the crossing from Monterey to Macao. When they reached 19° north latitude, they encountered heavy rains. Before long the heat became stifling and the humidity was extreme. La Pérouse redoubled his efforts to keep his crews healthy during this critical period when they suddenly moved from a cold to a hot and humid climate. Every morning he had coffee served to the men at breakfast. He ordered between-decks dried and aired and ordered the sailors to wash their shirts in rain water.

The storms and heavy seas finally ended around November 15, when the sky became perfectly clear. This lovely, tranquil weather remained with the frigates all the way to the equator, which they crossed on November 21 for the third time since they left Brest. As they progressed farther into the southern hemisphere, the seabirds became more numerous. The crews took them for heralds of land, after which their patience began to wear thin. Nevertheless, although visibility was perfect, no island came into sight. After they had passed 6° latitude, west winds and a heavy swell made sailing very difficult. On December 2, they passed the position assigned by Commodore Byron[1] to the Danger Islands. La Pérouse thought that he should take advantage of the west winds to visit the Samoan Islands (the Navigators of Bougainville)[2] where he could expect to find the fresh provisions which he most urgently needed.

On December 6, they sighted the easternmost island of this archipelago. Steering for it, on the following day they sighted its southern end. They did not see any canoes until they were in the channel. A large group of savages, seated in circles under coconut trees, seemed to be watching the frigates without any show of emotion and did not follow them. This island has an elevation of over six hundred feet, very steep cliffs, and is covered with large trees. The French exchanged some goods of little value with the islanders and soon discovered that, like other South Sea natives, these are signally lacking in good faith in their transactions.

They continued sailing in order to double a point behind which they expected to find a sheltered position, but it was impossible to locate an anchorage there. They then steered outside of the channel, intending to go along the two islands to the west, which together are almost as large as the easternmost island. A channel about six hundred feet wide separates these two islands, and at their western end the French sighted an islet which they would have taken for a large rock except that it was covered with trees.

---

[1] John Byron (1723–1786), an English navigator, born at Newstead Abbey, discovered a number of islands in the South Pacific.

[2] Louis de Bougainville explored the Pacific between 1766 and 1769. He made some of the most important French discoveries and named the Samoan Islands the Navigators Archipelago.

The next day they sighted a much larger island, that of Mauna [probably Tutuila]. Although they were three leagues from land, three or four canoes bringing pigs and fruit came alongside the frigates. This gave La Pérouse a most favorable opinion of the wealth of the island, which, as a matter of fact, is very large, well populated, and very fertile. So many advantages made it less difficult to choose an anchorage, and he gave the order to drop anchor in front of Mauna, on the open coast, in thirty fathoms.

The same evening, Captain de Langle, embarking with several officers in three armed boats, went to look at a populous village, where he received a very friendly welcome. Since it was late in the evening, the natives were obliging enough to light a great fire to illuminate the landing area for their visitors. Everything went well in this first meeting, and the boats returned to the ships.

The next day at sunrise, the natives came on board to trade, exchanging food for ironware and especially for glass beads, which pleased them very much. The longboats went ashore for water, and the two captains followed them in their boats. Relations with the natives were less friendly on this day. Some of the sailors who were ordered to form a cordon around the fresh water at the longboats allowed some women to pass through their line, and a savage who had slipped in behind the longboats hit one of the sailors with a mallet which he had seized. Instead of severely punishing the aggressor, La Pérouse merely had him thrown into the water. He should have acted much more rigorously in order to command the respect of these sturdy, powerful people who exaggerated their physical superiority and derided the slim figures of the strangers. He should have demonstrated the power of the French and the effect of their firearms other than by killing one or two pigeons in the air.

Nevertheless, La Pérouse and several armed men went to visit the village, which is shaded by groves of fruit trees. The houses are built around a lovely, circular green, almost three hundred yards in diameter. Standing in front of the doors of their homes, all the savages—men, women, children, old people—begged La Pérouse to honor them by his visit. He entered several houses. Each has a floor of pebbles selected for the purpose, raised two feet above the ground and covered with well-made mats. They are generally elliptical in form and have a row of tree trunks which support a roof made of palm leaves. In most cases, the interiors are perfectly neat and clean. To keep out the extreme heat of the sun, some homes have delicate mats, skillfully made to overlap like fish scales, which can be raised and lowered like our shutters. This delightful country, furthermore, has the double advantage of soil which is fertile without being cultivated and a climate which does not require any clothing. Breadfruit, coconuts, bananas, guava, and oranges provide these fortunate people with plenty of food. They also possess tame pigeons, charming turtledoves, and handsome parrots. What a picture of paradise this fortunate land presents! But it did not take the French long to discover that this was not the land of innocence. Great wounds—some scars, others still bleeding—betrayed the warlike, violent habits of these savages, and their features expressed the same fierceness.

While the captains were ashore, this aggressiveness was revealed more clearly on board the frigates. Despite the watchfulness of the guards, some of the savages had slipped up onto the deck and had stolen various articles here and there. Such transgressions should have been stopped by force, but these herculean fellows ridiculed the short Frenchmen and laughed at their threats. Our superiority should have been demonstrated by effective action, but this was not done. La Pérouse had to learn by experience which cost the frigates dearly.

It seemed as if fate led Captain de Langle into the disastrous sequence which cost him his life. During the day of December 10, he had noticed a pretty village in a nearby cove, and he wanted to return to it the next day, despite the reluctance of La Pérouse. Toward noon on the 11th, the two longboats of the frigates and the two pinnaces, carrying sixty-one picked men under de Langle's command, left the anchorage to go to the watering-place which this officer had seen the previous day. Instead of the spacious and convenient bay which he thought he had found, de Langle came upon a coral-filled cove which could be entered only by a narrow, winding channel. The captain, who had observed this bay at high tide, was not aware that the tide in these islands rises five or six feet. At first he wanted to turn back and go to the first watering-place, which had every advantage, but the friendly attitude of the natives waiting on the shore with a great supply of fruit and pigs reassured him, and he went on. They unloaded the water casks, established a cordon of soldiers to protect the shore party, and the work began peacefully. During the first hour, since the number of natives scarcely exceeded two hundred, there was no danger for de Langle with the means of defense which he had available. Numerous canoes, however, gradually came in from every direction, and soon fifteen hundred islanders covered the beach and crowded about the little creek, causing disorder and confusion. To put an end to it, de Langle hit upon the unfortunate device of distributing gifts to men whom he thought were chiefs. His generosity satisfied no one, neither the natives who benefited from it nor those who did not receive anything. On the contrary, the latter fell into a rage of jealousy, and from that moment a conflict became inevitable.

De Langle ordered his men to withdraw to the longboats. The savages did not interfere but merely entered the water and followed the French, who had to walk some distance through the water to reach their boats. During this movement, their muskets and cartridges became wet. All remained calm until the order was given to raise the grapples and shove off. At that moment, some stones were thrown, and de Langle replied with a musket shot fired into the air, which was the signal for a general attack by the natives. A hail of stones, thrown at very short range with the force of a sling, struck almost everybody in the longboat. The captain himself was knocked down and fell over the port side of the boat where more than two hundred savages rushed upon him and killed him with their clubs. When he was dead, the furious natives tied his body to the longboat in order to be certain of plundering his remains. Others who were surprised at the same time and were struck down with their commander were the naturalist Lamanon, the master-at-arms Talin, and several sailors. From every side swarms of savages fanned out into the water, scattering in all directions and offering a poor target to the swivel guns and muskets. Attacked from right and left, from front and rear, the crews no longer knew whom to obey nor how to defend themselves. It was a frightful battle, a bloody and confused clash in which the superiority of firearms was nullified by the situation.

It was impossible for the men to shove the longboats off into deep

Murder of de Langle, Lamanon, and ten members of the two crews

water and at the same time to defend themselves against the attacks of the natives. Lieutenant Boutin, in command of the second longboat, ordered his men to fire. At a range of four or five paces every musket shot could kill a savage, but there was no time to reload. The longboats were therefore abandoned, and the men managed to rejoin the pinnaces, which fortunately were still afloat. This move diverted the enemy. Carried away by their lust for plunder, the savages rushed upon the boats which had been abandoned to them and fought each other fiercely over the most worthless trifles, for all the world like a flock of scavenger birds pouncing upon a carcass. In a few minutes, the boats were ripped apart and there remained only the fragments—benches, oars, nails, rigging, and hardware. Engaged in this work of destruction, the aggressors forgot the fleeing sailors. The latter reached the pinnaces and jettisoned the water casks in order to lighten the craft and make room for everybody, then they steered for the open water. At the narrowest part of the entrance, however, another mishap almost sealed the fate of the unlucky men. The *Astrolabe*'s boat ran aground. The situation was critical. On both sides of the channel, and not more than ten feet away, the reef enabled the islanders to close in for another attack upon the retreating sailors. Furthermore, they had finished plundering the longboats, and now the raging mob, excited by their first victory, were ready for another. Yelling ferociously, the natives rushed forward in the expectation of more plunder and tried to cut off the French withdrawal, but several well-aimed volleys saved our sailors from a second disaster. The boats cleared the reef and returned to the frigates.

When the pinnaces with their cargo of wounded came alongside and those on board the frigates heard the tragic news of what had just happened, a loud cry for vengeance rose among the crews. Around the ships were a hundred canoes where the natives were selling supplies with an air of confidence which proved their innocence. These were the brothers, children, and fellow countrymen of the barbarians who had just committed the most heinous crime. They could provide a fitting sacrifice to be offered to the shades of the slain. The soldiers had already leaped to their cannon and weapons, but La Pérouse, always merciful, stopped these natural moves for vengeance. He had them fire a cannon, without shot, only once in order to dispel the canoes. In less than an hour, the natives had all disappeared.

La Pérouse at first planned to send out another party in retaliation for the crime committed upon his men and to recover the remains of the longboats. With this in mind, he approached the coast in search of an anchorage, but he found only the same coral bottom as de Langle had and a swell rolling toward land and breaking on the reefs. Furthermore, he gave in to the recommendations of Lieutenant Boutin, who pointed out that the situation in the bay was such that if the boats had the misfortune of running aground not a single man would come back alive because the trees, which extend to the water's edge, would provide the savages with cover from the musket fire while the French, after leaving their boats, would be exposed to a hail of stones.

It must have been with a painful effort that the captain wrenched himself away from the scene of tragedy and abandoned the bodies of his murdered comrades, especially of his old friend, a man of courage, judgment, and understanding, and one of the best officers in the French navy. After two days of futile endeavor, with a heart full of sadness, he had to resign himself to leaving this tragic place, which was given the name Massacre Island.

On December 13 the order to get under way was issued, and they headed for the island of Oiolava [Upolu], separated from Mauna by a channel about nine leagues wide. Tahiti can scarcely compare with it in beauty, dimensions, fertility, and population. When they had come within three leagues of its northwest point, the frigates were surrounded by a countless number of canoes laden with provisions of every kind. The savages who manned them are of the same physical type as those of Mauna, but their manners are gentler, and the trading went on with a great deal more tranquillity. In the evening, the frigates hove to opposite the village, perhaps the largest on any island in the South Seas. It occupies a broad plain covered with houses from the foot of the mountain to the water's edge. These mountains are almost in the center of the island. From there the land descends in a gradual slope, so that to those on board the ships it looked like an amphitheater covered with trees, houses, and vegetation. They saw the smoke rising from the middle of the village as it does over the center of a large city, and they saw the sea covered with countless canoes, attracted partly by curiosity and partly by a desire to trade with the Europeans. These savages have no knowledge of iron; they always refuse to accept it, and they prefer a single glass bead to a hatchet. They are well supplied with the necessities of life, and in trading demand only some of the superfluities. Among a rather large number of women, La Pérouse noticed two or three of attractive appearance. Their hair, adorned with flowers and a fillet of green ribbon, is braided with grass and moss; their figures are exquisite; their eyes, expressions, and motions manifest mildness, as much as the men in theirs express fierceness and deceit.

At nightfall, the expedition resumed its course along the island, and the canoes returned to land. The next day, they sailed along the island of Pola [Savaii], much closer in than on the previous occasion. There the islanders probably knew of the Mauna massacre, since no canoes came out to visit the frigates. Somewhat smaller but as beautiful, Pola is separated from the populous island of Oiolava by a channel about four leagues wide, which in turn is divided by two fairly large islands, one of which, being very low and heavily wooded, is probably inhabited. The northern coast of Pola, like that of the other islands in this archipelago, is inaccessible to ships. Not until the French had doubled the island's western point did they find the sea calm and smooth, a condition which promised excellent roadsteads.

Bougainville's Navigators Archipelago, consisting of seven islands located at 14° south latitude and between 171° and 175° west longitude, is one of the most beautiful groups in the South Seas. The inhabitants are robust, handsome people; almost all of them are five feet nine, ten, or eleven inches tall; their height, however, is less amazing than the heroic proportions of their limbs. The men paint or tattoo their bodies so that they seem to be clothed even though they are almost naked. Their only apparel is a band worn around the waist and made of aquatic grass which reaches to their knees and reminded the French of the rivers of mythology described as covered with reeds. They wear their hair very long, often tying it up around the head, thus adding to the fierceness of their appearance. The women are as statuesque as the men.

These people have achieved a high degree of skill in the practice of certain arts. We saw how much artistry they use in constructing their homes. For a few glass beads, they sold the French large wooden tripod platters made of a single block and so highly polished they seemed to be lacquered. They also make very fine mats and some fabrics of paper and linen which the chiefs wind around their body like a skirt. Their language is a dialect of that spoken in the Society Islands and in the Friendly Islands.

Among fifteen to eighteen hundred islanders observed by the French, at least thirty claimed to be chiefs. They exercise a kind of police power and use a stick to strike those in their entourage. Never were rulers less obeyed nor the orders which they gave so quickly violated. Aptly named the Navigators by Bougainville, they always travel by canoe and never go on foot from one village to another. All the villages are located in coves along the coast and have footpaths leading only into the interior of the country. La Pérouse did not see any *marae* (tomb), nor was he able to witness any of their religious ceremonies.

CHAPTER X

Niue Islands (Cocos and Traitors Islands)
Arrival at the Tonga Islands (Friendly Islands)
Relations with the Inhabitants of Tongatabu
Norfolk Island—Arrival at Botany Bay

LA PÉROUSE came in close to observe the great splendid island of Pola, but he had no contact with the natives, since his crews were still too hot with anger for a stop to be feasible. After doubling the western shore of the island, no other land could be seen. On December 21, he sighted two islands immediately recognized as the Niue Islands[1] (Schouten's[2] Cocos [Tafahi or Boscawen] and Traitors [Niuatoputapu or Keppel] Islands). The first is shaped like a very high sugarloaf. Covered with trees to the top, it is almost one league in diameter and is separated from Traitors Island by a strait about three miles wide. The latter is low and flat with only a hill near the center. It is divided into two parts by a channel about three hundred yards wide at the entrance.

They brought the ships to about two miles from a large bay on the western side of Traitors Island. Twenty canoes immediately came out to the frigates in order to begin trading. They were loaded with exceptionally fine coconuts and other local products, making it obvious that the natives of these islands had already traded with Europeans. They seemed to be an ill-natured, unsociable lot, and each one was minus two phalanges on

---

[1] Not to be confused with the island of Niue to the southeast.
[2] Willem Cornelis Schouten was a Dutch mariner who crossed the Pacific with Jacob Lemaire in 1615–1616.

the little finger of the right hand. Every island in this region reminded the French of the natives' treachery. Roggeveen's[3] crew had been stoned at Creation Island, to the east of the Samoan Islands; Schouten's men had experienced the same treatment on Traitors Island, which could be seen from the frigates at that time; and their own companions had just been murdered at Mauna. These considerations had a direct effect upon their policy toward the savages. They used force against the slightest thefts and wrongdoings; they refused to allow the natives to come aboard; they threatened to kill those who, nevertheless, dared to board the ships. This conduct, so different from the policy of moderation which they had previously followed, gained the respect of the natives of Traitors Island.

On December 23, while they were trading coconuts with the savages, they were struck by a violent squall which scattered the canoes. Several capsized, and after being righted they quickly reached land. Although the weather was threatening, the French, nevertheless, circled the island in order to observe all the points and make an exact map. La Pérouse then steered for the Tonga or Friendly Islands with the intention of reconnoitering those which Captain Cook did not have time to explore.

Meanwhile, the humidity was causing great distress among all who had symptoms of scurvy. This disease was not widespread among the seamen, but it attacked many of the officers and their servants who were unaccustomed to life at sea and were unable to tolerate the lack of fresh provisions. David, the cook, died on December 10 from the ravages of this dread disease. To protect his crew against it, La Pérouse had them drink spruce beer. Each man received a daily ration of one bottle of it, and also a half-pint of wine, and an allowance of brandy mixed with water. At the same time, they received two daily allowances of fresh pork provided by the pigs bought at Mauna. The new diet had a refreshing effect on the men, and the swelling in the legs and the other scurvy symptoms disappeared.

The north-northwest winds always brought rain and often were as hard as the west winds which blow upon the Brittany coast. On December

---

[3] Jacob Roggeveen, a Dutch admiral, sailed around the world in 1721–1722 and discovered Easter Island and some of the northern islands of the Tuamotu archipelago. He is credited also with sighting some of the Samoan Islands.

27 Vavau Island was sighted. This island, which Captain Cook did not visit, although he was told of it by the inhabitants of Tonga, is one of the largest of the Friendly Islands. The honor of discovering it belongs to the Spaniard Maurelle, who explored it in 1781 during his crossing from Manila to San Blas on the west coast of Mexico.

During the day of the 27th, La Pérouse tacked to and fro in order to approach Vavau. After pursuing his northward tack during the night in order to extend his observations twelve to fifteen leagues beyond the island, he sighted Maurelle's Amargura Island. After taking its bearings, he ordered a course for Vavau, which was visible only from the top of the masts. They were soon at the entrance of the harbor where the navigator Maurelle had anchored, but since the admiral was in a hurry to reach Botany Bay, he merely brought the ships near enough to land to take the island's bearings and to make contact with the islanders. The weather was so bad and the sky so threatening that no canoe came out to the frigates. La Pérouse next steered for Late Island, included in the list of the Tonga Islands compiled by Captain Cook. He came within two miles of it, quite certain that no canoe would risk the sea in such foul weather. At this island a squall struck the ships, forcing them to move toward Kao and Tofoa, which were discovered by Cook in 1774 and seen again by Maurelle in 1781. Kao is a very high island, well populated, and nine miles in circumference. As for Tofoa, it is also high but with a small population and capped by an active volcano.

After observing these two volcanic islands, La Pérouse maintained his course and raised two rocky islets, Hunga Tonga and Hunga Haapai, about two miles apart. Shaggy with brush to their tops, they serve as sentinels informing travelers that they have come to Tongatabu. Finally on December 31, the lookouts sighted the heart of the archipelago, a fertile country, not very high but covered with luxuriant vegetation. La Pérouse ordered a course to the southern point of the island, which they were able to approach within a distance of three musket shots. The sea was breaking furiously upon the whole coast, but beyond the breakers they saw the most delightful orchards.

The island homes are not grouped in villages but are scattered in the fields, like the homesteads on the best cultivated plains of Europe. Seven or eight canoes were soon launched upon the sea and came toward the frigates, but the natives manning them were timid sailors; although the sea was very pleasant, they did not dare to approach closer than fifty or sixty feet from the frigates, which had hove to. Then they leaped into the water and brought their coconuts, which they traded for pieces of iron, nails, and small hatchets. Their canoes are exactly like those of the Samoan Islanders except that they are not equipped with sails. Complete confidence was quickly established between the natives and the visitors. Thus emboldened, they came aboard. The French, who had read the reports of Cook's voyages, spoke to them about Poulaho, Feenou, and some other chiefs.[4] The natives reacted like old acquaintances meeting again and speaking of their friends. A young islander indicated that he was Feenou's son, and this claim, whether true or usurped, was worth several gifts. He shouted with glee every time he received one, and by means of sign language tried to make the travelers understand that if they should anchor on the coast they would find there an ample supply of provisions and that the canoes were too small to bring them out upon the open sea. These savages are boisterous but not ferocious. Their language, tattooing, and clothing all indicate that they have the same origin as the natives of the Samoan Islands. The custom of cutting off the two bones of the little finger, as a sign of mourning for the loss of a relative or friend, is as common among these people as at Niue.

Cautious and careful now, La Pérouse was unwilling to risk a landing. His relations with the natives of Tongatabu consisted merely of visits on their part.[5] On January 1, 1788, having learned that as long as he tacked

---

[4] In May, 1777, Cook was at Nomuka Island where he met Feenou, chief of Tongatabu, and at the Haapai group where he was introduced to Poulaho, the king of the Friendly Islands. Poulaho then invited Cook to visit Tongatabu, where Cook remained until July 10.

[5] Since La Pérouse received only a few Tonga Island natives on board his ship, he did not have time to observe these islanders, whom he expected to visit again later on. The following details, provided by recent travelers, will fill the gap in his report.

The inhabitants of the Tonga Islands have a complexion similar to that of the people of southern Europe, an aquiline nose, thin lips, straight hair, and are tall and well proportioned. Their appearance is pleasant, their demeanor dignified and respectable. The temperature of their climate, and healthy, abundant nourishment generally

about on the open sea he would not obtain enough fresh provisions for his crew, La Pérouse decided to steer a course for Botany Bay, on the coast of Australia (New Holland). Furthermore, he needed to build new long-boats to replace those which had been lost. Before noon on the 2nd, he sighted Pylstaart Island, the widest part of which measures a quarter of a league. It is very steep, with only a few trees on the shore, and can be of no use except as a resting place for seabirds.

The frigates were becalmed for three days, within sight of this island rock. The sun, which was at its zenith, made these calms a hundred times more irksome for the sailors than contrary winds. La Pérouse noticed

---

keep them in a satisfactory state of health; they are, however, vulnerable to certain diseases, such as leprosy, elephantiasis, marasmus, and skin disorders.

Their character contains striking paradoxes; they can be kind and cruel at the same time, generous and greedy, gracious and deceptive; they can entertain their guests and murder them, but what is most remarkable is their bravery and mental ability. Their understanding of crime is limited to violations of tabu and disobedience to the chiefs. They spend their time in much the same way as we, for example in caring for their property, in games, dancing, and pleasant conversation. They are almost always interested in discussing the *Papa-Languis* or Europeans who have visited them. Among the many skilled trades which they practice must be mentioned the construction of houses and canoes, making necklaces from the teeth of the sperm whale, building vaults for the burial of chiefs, fishing with nets and hooks, tattooing, and carving war clubs.

The clothing of these islanders consists of fine matting or cloth, which they wrap around the body, winding it one and a half times around the waist and holding it with a belt. For the head, they have a small cap or length of cloth wound like a turban or sometimes simply a visor of woven coconut palms to shade the eyes from the sun. Some wear their hair long and loose, others cut it close; still others dye their hair white or red and then curl it with the greatest care. Both men and women are meticulous in keeping their bodies clean.

Their weapons are lances and all types of war clubs. After Europeans began to visit their islands, the natives obtained a number of muskets from them and many bayonets which they attached to long sticks.

They have various musical instruments, including a kind of drum and a flute made of bamboo closed at both ends and having six openings which are blown into with the nose. As in Tahiti and the Hawaiian Islands, these people have national songs. Some of these chants relate their history from the earliest times, others are used as accompaniment to their dances, which are graceful, refined, and varied.

By religion these islanders are animists, since they worship *hotouas*, which are vague and ill-defined spirits.—Valentin

that in general the trade winds are irregular in this part of the world. Norfolk Island and the two islets off its southern point were sighted on the 13th. La Pérouse dropped anchor one mile from land. A heavy sea was breaking around the island, but he believed that his boats would find a sheltered place behind the great rocks which bordered the shore. He therefore directed Captain Clonard to take four boats to land but not to risk a landing if there was the slightest danger of the waves capsizing them. The captain proceeded a half league without finding a spot where a landing could be made. He saw that the island is encircled by a rampart formed by lava which had flowed from the top of the mountain and which, cooled by its downward course, had left in many places an overhang that projected several feet over the shore. Had a landing been possible, the party could have penetrated into the interior of the island only by working its way up some very swiftly flowing torrents which had formed ravines. Beyond these natural barriers, the island is covered with pines and carpeted with luxuriant grass. From his deck, La Pérouse followed the boats' movements, and when he saw through his telescope that they did not find a suitable landing place he signaled them to return. A short time later he gave the order to get under way.

They then pressed sail for Botany Bay, which was not more than three hundred leagues distant. At twilight on January 14, the rear admiral gave the signal to heave to and take soundings to a depth of two hundred fathoms. The configuration of the bottom in the vicinity of Norfolk Island made him believe that the depth remained the same all the way to Australia. That this supposition was false he discovered as he continued on his course. He made considerable headway by day but very little by night, since the course which he was taking had never been navigated by any previous explorer.

On January 23, the Australian coast was sighted; a low-lying country, it can hardly be seen at a distance of over twelve leagues. The winds then became very variable so that the day of the 24th was spent tacking back and forth in sight of Botany Bay without being able to double Point Solander, which remained a league to the north. There was a strong wind from that direction, and the ships were not good enough sailers to overcome the force of the wind and of the currents.

The same day, the French witnessed a sight such as they had not seen since they left Manila. This novelty was an English fleet anchored in Botany Bay. Even the pennants and flags were visible. Here was Commodore Phillip, escorted by the *Sirius* and the *Supply*. He had just laid the foundations of the colony later to become widely known as New South Wales.[6] All Europeans are fellow countrymen when they meet so far from home, and the French were most impatient to reach their anchorage. They were unable, however, to accomplish this until January 26. La Pérouse had the most pleasant relations with the English officers, who offered him every possible assistance and gave him a detailed explanation

---

[6] Toward the end of the last century, the English were looking for a place to which they could deport their convicts. Thanks to Banks, they thought of Australia and Botany Bay, which this naturalist had visited on his first voyage with Cook. The first attempt took place in 1787. Nine ships were equipped to carry the convicts, their guards, and supplies to the new colony. The frigate *Sirius* and the brig *Supply* were to protect the convoy, and Commodore Phillip, the first governor of the penal colony, flew his flag from the frigate. This squadron brought out one thousand seventeen persons, including five hundred sixty-five male prisoners, one hundred ninety-two female prisoners, and the various persons responsible for the administration and protection of the colony.

After departing from England, May 13, 1787, the squadron arrived in the roadstead of Botany Bay, January 20, 1788. As soon as he had dropped anchor, Phillip recognized the country described by Banks. He soon learned that it was unsuitable for a settlement, and he had to go several miles north to drop anchor in front of Port Jackson. Here they founded the city of Sydney, the colony's original name. The initial stages of a settlement of this kind were bound to be difficult. English persistence never faltered. Land was given to soldiers who were willing to do manual labor in order to improve their lot.

The colony eventually began to prosper. For a long time hostile to the intruders, the native tribes finally accepted them and made peace. Land was cleared on a very large scale. The harvests grew greater and greater, and the animals brought from Europe multiplied until they were numberless. A regular administration was organized for the cities of Sydney and Paramata. Magistrates, constables, and watchmen were appointed; churches, schools, hospitals, and prisons were built. The young colony grew so rapidly that it now includes several well ordered municipalities. Considering the origin of New South Wales and the progress made there during the past half century, plaudits are definitely due the colonial genius of the English people, while we French must vow to achieve as much in our recently conquered Algeria.— Valentin

of the purpose of their expedition. Commodore Phillip agreed to deliver the French admiral's reports to France.

La Pérouse's account of his voyage ends at this point. It does not contain a description of his stay on the Australian coast because he was accustomed to write his journal only after putting out to sea. The last news of him was received from Botany Bay. The dispatches which he sent from there to Europe contained a letter to the Minister of the Navy describing the course he was going to follow. After leaving Botany Bay, he planned to return to the Tonga Islands, next to explore certain parts of New Caledonia, the Louisiade group, and the Solomon Islands, and then to pass through Torres Strait in order to reach Mauritius toward the end of 1788. On the basis of these statements, gallant d'Entrecasteaux undertook, as described in the appendix, to trace the missing expedition. His devotion to duty in this task deserved a happier ending.

 SUPPLEMENT

*Description of the Natives
of the Various Islands Explored by La Pérouse*

LA PÉROUSE was not the only member of his expedition who recorded the events of the voyage and its experiences ashore. Almost all of the officers kept diaries in which they recorded their impressions and observations of the uncivilized peoples whom they visited. Of these reports, one in particular stands out by reason of the accuracy of the descriptions and the attention given to details. This is the journal of Rollin, ship's surgeon on the *Boussole*. Selections from the various reports written by this officer form a useful complement to the narrative of the expedition's commander.

Easter Island and Maui

Easter Island is not so barren and forbidding as other travelers have described it. That the island is almost unforested is true, but its hills and dales are covered with pleasant vegetation. The size and excellence of the yams, sweet potatoes, and sugar cane are signs of the island's fertility and the vigor of its plant life.

Equally inexact are the descriptions of the natives given by certain navigators. Roggeveen's giants are nowhere to be found nor are the weak, undernourished individuals reported by a contemporary traveler. On the contrary, I saw a numerous population, better endowed with grace and beauty than any of those whom I later had occasion to meet. The soil easily provides them with excellent food in more than enough quantity for their needs, although fresh water is scarce and of an inferior quality.

These islanders are moderately stout, with a pleasant figure and appearance. Of well-proportioned stature, they are about five feet four inches tall. Except for their complexions, their features look the same as those of Europeans. They are tawny-skinned, with black hair; some, however, have light-colored hair. They have the custom of painting themselves, tattooing their skin, and piercing their ears; they widen this opening with sugar cane leaves rolled into a spiral until the ear lobes reach the shoulders. Since this condition is a mark of distinction, the men strive to achieve it.

These people seem to live in the most complete anarchy. As far as we could determine, there is no chief. Both men and women go almost naked; a few, however, wear a piece of cloth which they wrap around their shoulders or hips and which reaches halfway down their thighs.

These islanders are not unskilled. Their houses, for example, are quite large and perfectly built according to their requirements. They are made of reeds supported by small rafters, forming a vault about fifty feet long and ten or twelve feet wide, the highest point being ten or twelve feet above the ground. On the sides there are several entrances, not more than three feet in diameter. The interior is not remarkable in any way. We saw only some mats, which they lay out upon the ground for sleeping, and some small household goods. Their cloth is made from the paper mulberry. They also make hats, reed baskets, and wooden figurines, which evidenced a fair degree of skill.

The only animals we found on Easter Island were chickens, and, of all the wild animals, rats are the only quadrupeds there. We saw very few seabirds, and concluded that fish are scarce in the local waters.

The eastern part of the island has a very large crater which, on its seaward side, is almost completely surrounded with a great number of statues or crude busts on which only the eyes, nose, mouth, and ears had been roughly carved. At the base of these statues are the mysterious caves mentioned in Cook's report. These hypogea provide each family with a burial place for its dead.

Since La Pérouse had already given many presents to the islanders, he wanted to prove his good wishes to them in another way and to promote their welfare in a more lasting manner. He therefore left several domesticated animals on the island and had his men plant every kind of fruit and vegetable there.

After performing these acts of good will, we set sail on a course for the Hawaiian Islands. When we were in sight of Maui, one of the islands of this archipelago, about two hundred canoes came out from the shore to meet the frigates. All the canoes were loaded with pigs, fruits, and fresh vegetables which the natives conveyed to us on board and forced us to accept as gifts. The wind then became stronger and speeded us on our way, preventing us from taking full advantage of these generous offers and from further enjoying both the picturesque view of the island and the great gathering of canoes, which, as they moved about, provided us with the most exhilarating and exciting scenic spectacle imaginable.

We dropped anchor on the west side of Maui on May 29, 1786. This part of the island does not have nearly as much vegetation nor as many people as we had noticed on the eastern side where we had landed. Nevertheless, we had scarcely anchored before we were surrounded by the natives who brought us pigs, fruits, and vegetables in their canoes. We began trading with so much success that in a few hours we had on board nearly three hundred pigs and an adequate supply of vegetables which cost only several pieces of iron. If Maui amply provides its people with animals and all the necessities of life, these islanders are nevertheless very far from enjoying as good health as those of Easter Island, where there are fewer and less abundant natural resources. The Hawaiians are also less endowed with grace and beauty than the latter. Their average height is about five feet three inches; they are somewhat less fleshy, and they have coarse features, thick eyebrows, black eyes which without being hard express self-confidence, prominent cheekbones, slightly widened nostrils, thick lips, a large mouth, and teeth which are somewhat wide but quite fine and straight. Their hair is black and cut in the pattern of a helmet. Worn very long, like the flowing crest of a helmet, their hair is a reddish-brown color at the ends. This color is probably produced by the acid juice of some plant.

These people paint and tattoo their skin. They pierce their ears and nasal septa, and adorn themselves with rings inserted in these parts. Their clothing consists of a piece of fabric wrapped around the body. The cloth made by these islanders from the bark of the paper mulberry is excellent and diverse. They dye it very artistically, their designs being so exact that they seem to have been imitating our printed calicos. Their houses, grouped in villages, are built in the same way as those of Easter Island but in the form of a square. The most obvious feature of the social structure of the people of Maui is their division into several tribes, each of which is ruled by a chief.

On the American Indians Who Live in the Vicinity of Frenchmen's Bay
These people seem to have little in common with the natives of California. They are larger and sturdier, better looking and dynamically expressive; they are also very superior in intelligence and in spirit. They have a somewhat low forehead, with less hair than the southern Amerinds. All of them have very lively, black eyes; rather heavy eyebrows; a large, straight nose only slightly widened at the end; slightly fleshy lips, a mouth of average size, fine, straight teeth, and very regular chin and ears. The women share these physical advantages, and they would even be quite attractive if they did not have the custom of piercing and stretching their lower lips by inserting in the opening a kind of small wooden bowl which they consider an adornment but which makes them hideous in European eyes.

These people have an olive complexion, but their nails, which they keep long, are of a lighter shade. We noticed that some individuals have a much lighter skin color, the same being true of the parts of the body which are not exposed to the action of the sun and the atmosphere.

Their hair is generally not so coarse and dark as that of the southern Amerinds; many of them have brown hair. They also have a thicker beard.

The perfect regularity of their teeth caused me to believe that this was accomplished artificially, but upon close, careful examination, I discovered that the enamel had not been altered and that this regularity was natural.

These people paint their faces and bodies, they tattoo themselves, and pierce their ears and nasal septa.

The Natives of Sakhalin Island and Eastern Tartary

On July 12, 1787, we dropped anchor in De Langle Bay, located on the western side of Choka or Sakhalin Island.

The following day we went ashore, and as soon as we were on land the natives came to us and sought to demonstrate their good will toward us, thus leading us to believe that our dealing with them would be profitable.

These people are very intelligent, they respect property, they are trusting and have no difficulty communicating with strangers. They are of medium height, heavy set, with powerful physiques, a tendency to corpulence, and well-developed muscles and figures. The average height of these islanders is five feet, and the maximum height is five feet four inches; men this tall are very rare.

All of them have large heads and broad faces, which are rounder than those of Europeans. Their appearance and expression are quite pleasant and lively, although their general facial composition does not meet our standards of beauty. Almost all have large cheeks; a short, round nose with very thick outer walls; well-shaped, sparkling eyes of average size, blue in some people and black in most; full eyebrows, a medium-sized mouth, a strong voice, and thick, red lips. We noticed that some individuals have blue tattooing on the middle of their lips. Like their eyes, their lips were capable of expressing every kind of emotion. They usually have a full set of fine, regular teeth, a rounded and slightly prominent chin, and small ears. These they pierce and adorn with glass jewelry or silver rings.

The women have their upper lips entirely tattooed in blue; their hair is worn long. They wear exactly the same clothing as the men; both sexes have tawny-colored skin; their nails, which they keep long, are a darker shade than those of the Europeans. The long, full beards of the islanders give to them and in particular to the old men an air of dignity and venerability. The young people seem to have great respect and consideration for these old men. Their hair is black, glossy, and moderately copious; some people have brown hair, and all wear it rolled, about six inches long in the back and cropped along the forehead and at the temples.

Their clothing consists of a gown or kind of kimono which overlaps in front where it is held fast by small buttons, strings, and by a sash tied above the hips. This gown is made of skin or quilted nankeen, a cloth the natives make from willow bark. The garment usually reaches down to the calves and sometimes farther, thus making it unnecessary in most cases for them to wear any other clothing. Some wear sealskin boots which, in the form of the foot and in the workmanship, resemble Chinese footwear. Most of them, however, go barefoot and bareheaded. Only a small number wear a band of bearskin wound around the head, but they use this as an ornament rather than for protection against the effects of the cold and the heat.

Like low-class Chinese, all of these people wear a belt to which they attach their knives for defense against bears, and various small sacks where they keep their tinderbox, their pipe, and their tobacco pouch, smoking being a widespread habit among them.

Their houses, while providing protection against rain and other inclement weather, are not large, considering the number of persons living in them. The roof forms two inclined planes rising to a height of about ten or twelve inches at their junction, three or four on the sides, and fourteen to fifteen feet in width by eighteen feet in length. These cabins are constructed with solidly joined rafters. The roofing and siding consist of tree bark and dried grass, arranged in the same way as the straw which covers the thatched cots of our peasants.

In the interior of these houses, we noticed a square of earth about six inches high and supported on the sides by small boards; this is the hearth. At the sides and in the rear of the apartment are trestle-beds, twelve to fifteen inches high. When it is time to retire the natives lay sleeping mats out upon these.

The utensils used for preparing and serving their food consist of iron pots and bowls or containers made in various ways and shapes of wood and birch bark. Like the Chinese, they eat with chopsticks. Every family has its meals at noon and toward the end of the day.

The homes in the southern part of the island are somewhat more elaborately finished and decorated. They have wooden floors, and their decorations include Japanese porcelain vases to which the householders are greatly attached, leading us to believe that the vases are very expensive and difficult to obtain. They do not raise any crops but live on fish, which is smoked and dried in the open, and on whatever game they take by hunting.

Each family has its canoes and its hunting and fishing equipment. Their weapons are the bow, the javelin, and a kind of spontoon used especially in bear hunting. Next to their homes they have sheds where they store provisions which have been processed and stockpiled during good weather in preparation for the winter. The supplies consist of dried fish, great amounts of garlic and wild celery, angelica, a bulbous root locally called *ape* and elsewhere known as the Kamchatka yellow lily, and fish oil kept in bags made of the stomachs of large animals. These warehouses are well constructed of planks, completely enclosed, raised above the ground and supported by several stakes about four feet high.

As far as we saw, dogs are the only animals which the natives of Sakhalin have. They are of medium size, with somewhat long hair, upright ears, a long muzzle, and a bark which is loud but not fierce.

Of all the uncivilized peoples whom we have visited, these islanders, if they can still be included in the above category, are the only ones among whom we saw weavers' looms; although small enough to be portable, these are perfect looms. They use a spindle for spinning the hair of animals, willow bark, and the fibres of the common or great nettle. These are the threads they weave into their cloths.

These people, with their gentle, trusting character, seem to trade with the Chinese through the Tartars of Manchuria, with the Russians in the northern part of their island, and with the Japanese in the southern part. This commerce, however, is of little consequence, as it consists only of some furs and whale oil. Whaling is carried on only at the southern end of the island. The oil is extracted in an inefficient manner. The whale is dragged up on a sloping beach where it is allowed to decompose; the oil which separates out of it is collected in a kind of tub placed at the bottom of the incline, the flow being directed by small furrows.

The island, called Choka by its inhabitants, Ocu Jesso by the Japanese, and Sakhalin by the Russians, who are acquainted only with the northern part of it, extends along its long axis from the forty-sixth to the fifty-fourth parallel.

Well-wooded and high in the middle, it flattens out toward the ends, where the soil seems suitable for agriculture. The plant life is extremely vigorous; pines, willows, oaks, and birches fill the forests. The surrounding seas abound in fish, while the island's rivers and streams swarm with the finest salmon and trout.

The weather was very foggy and rather mild while we were there. All the natives I saw have a hardy, healthy-looking complexion, which they keep well into old age. I observed no serious deformity among them nor any trace of contagious or other diseases.

After having made a number of visits with the natives of Sakhalin Island, which was separated from the coast of Tartary by a strait presumed to connect the Sea of Japan with the Okhotsk Sea, we continued to travel northward. As the depth of the channel became progressively and constantly less until it was only six fathoms, La Pérouse decided that for the safety of his expedition he should turn back to the south, especially since we had virtually proved the impossibility of reaching Kamchatka by disemboguing northward. The persistent fogs, however, and the south winds, which prevailed almost constantly during the four months we were in these waters, placed us in a predicament, so that our progress southward was as tedious as it was difficult.

Since we had used up the wood and water taken on at Manila, our commander sought to replenish our stock of these commodities before attempting anything else.

On July 27, 1787, the weather cleared enough to allow us to sight a wide bay where we dropped anchor. It provided us a safe shelter against storms and a perfect opportunity to obtain the supplies we needed in order to continue our voyage. Located on the Tartary coast at 51° 29′ north latitude and 139° 41′ longitude, it was named De Castries Bay.

The country is very mountainous and so heavily wooded that the whole coast is one continuous forest. The plant life of the region is very luxuriant.

The inhabitants, who were the only people we saw on this coast since leaving Korea, had settled at the end of the bay near a small stream abounding in fish. These people are gentle, courteous, and like the Sakhalin Islanders, not at all aggressive toward strangers. They have the most scrupulous respect for the property of others and showed little curiosity or desire for getting articles which could be of the greatest use to them. Their method of greeting is a deep bow, and when they want to express great respect they kneel down until the forehead almost touches the ground.

In their external physical characteristics these people follow a definite pattern which has little in common with that of their neighbors, the inhabitants of Sakhalin, who are separated from them only by a strait ten to twelve leagues wide at this point.

The Tartars are shorter, smaller, and of a much less pleasing and less graceful appearance. Their complexions are somewhat lighter, and where the skin is always covered it is almost white; their hair is not so thick, and they have very little beard on the chin and upper lip. The Sakhalin Islanders, on the other hand, as I have stated, are well-knit, powerfully muscled, and hairier than most Europeans. The physical difference between these nations seems to indicate that they belong to different races, although they live in the same climate, and their manners and customs are similar, with only minor differences.

The women are homely. Their faces have none of the quality of gentleness which distinguishes women from men.

Most of the men are four feet nine or ten inches tall. The head is large in relation to the rest of the body, the face flat and almost square, the forehead small, rounded and slightly depressed from front to rear; eyebrows are thin, hair black or brown, eyes small, protruding, and so narrow that even when open the eyelids are never fully parted; nose is short with a slightly developed, almost indistinguishable base; cheeks heavy and prominent; mouth large with thick, red lips; teeth small, straight, but susceptible to decay; chin inconspicuous and lower jaw narrow; the limbs are small and spare of muscle. Because of the irregular development of all these parts, physical gracefulness and facial symmetry are lacking in these people, who are the homeliest, sorriest men I have seen in two hemispheres. Although these Tartars, as well as the inhabitants of Sakhalin, have achieved a fairly high degree of culture and civilization, they practice no husbandry and live in the greatest squalor. Their principal nourishment is fish, fresh during the summer and smoked during the winter. They dry the fish out in the open on racks somewhat like those used by our laundresses. After removing the head, they gut and bone the fish, then hang it on the rack. When the fish is dry, it is collected in heaps and stored in sheds like those used on Sakhalin Island.

The fish are caught on hooks and with nets or speared with a kind of spontoon or iron-tipped stick.

They are in the habit of sharing two meals together, one toward the middle of the day and the other in the evening. The cooking utensils and methods are the same as those of the natives of Sakhalin. They get these and other articles from Tartary, Manchuria, and Japan.

We were astonished to see the eagerness with which they eat the raw skin and the cartilaginous parts of the fresh fish, such as the snout and the area surrounding the gills. This treat and fish oil seemed to me to be the delicacies which they most prefer.

Men and women wear a smock like that of our teamsters or a kind of gown which reaches to the calves and is fastened in front with copper buttons. This clothing, which resembles that of the people of Sakhalin, is made of fish skin, sometimes of nankeen, and of the skins of land animals for winter wear. The women decorate the bottom of this garment with small copper plaques arranged in a pattern. Everybody also wears a kind of Chinese-style trousers and small boots similar to those worn on Sakhalin. They likewise have a horn or metal ring on the thumb and jewelry hanging from the ears and the side of the nose.

I discovered no other chiefs among them than the heads of each family. The only animals they raise are dogs of the same breed as those of Sakhalin; these they likewise use in winter for pulling sleds.

The climatic extremes of Tartary force the inhabitants to have different homes for winter and for summer. The design and furnishings of these are the same as those described in the discussion of Sakhalin. The winter homes have only one distinctive feature, which is that the floor is about four feet below the surface of the ground and the entry is reached through a kind of vestibule or entrance-hall.

Despite the dismal hardship of their way of life, these Tartars seem to enjoy moderately good health during their youth, but as they grow older they are afflicted with conjunctivitis, which is very common among them, and with blindness. These infirmities are most likely so frequent because they are brought on by general causes such as the radiance of the snow, which covers the land for more than half the year, and the continual irritating effect upon the eyes of the smoke which always fills their cabins, where they spend much of their time in the winter because of the cold and in the summer to escape the mosquitoes, which are extremely numerous in these latitudes. Skin diseases are very rare among these people despite the extreme squalor in which they live.

The occupations of both sexes, their hunting and fishing equipment, and their canoes are not noticeably different from those of the Sakhalin Islanders. Their physical capacity, however, makes them incapable of exerting the same efforts as the latter people, who are physically far more vigorous.

All these people seem to have the greatest respect for their dead, using all of their skill to give them a decent burial. The deceased are buried in their regular attire with the weapons and tools which served them during life. The bodies are placed in coffins made of boards in the same design as our own. The ends of the coffins are decorated with pieces of silk, plain or embroidered in gold or silver. The coffin is then enclosed in a tomb built of planks or boards and raised about four feet above the ground.

APPENDIX

D'Urville's Expedition to Vanikoro

THE FOLLOWING DATA have been borrowed from an important work, *Voyage de la Corvette L'Astrolabe, 1826–1829*, published by M. d'Urville,[1] concerning his voyage in search of La Pérouse, and from the journal of the expedition's artist, M. de Sainson, who has given us an accurate, incisive description of the site of the wreck, the discovery of the remains, and the erection of a simple memorial to our unfortunate fellow country-men. Until now [1875] this is the latest report available to navigators on the fate of the commander of the *Boussole* and the *Astrolabe*.

When the news from Botany Bay was not followed by later reports in 1789 and 1790, grave concern became widespread. Taking the initiative, the Society of Natural History requested the National Assembly to send an expedition in search of La Pérouse and his ships. This the Assembly generously voted to do by its decree of February 9, 1791, approved by Louis XVI. The necessary preparations for the expedition were ordered.

---

[1] Jules Sebastien Cesar Dumont d'Urville (1790–1842), born at Condé-sur-Noireau, made a voyage around the world, in the course of which he found the remains of the wreck of La Pérouse at Vanikoro. He explored part of the Antarctic region in 1838. In 1820, while engaged in a hydrographic survey of the Mediterranean, he recog-nized a recently unearthed statue as the Venus de Milo and reported it to the French ambassador at Constantinople. He died in a railroad accident near Meudon.

Two large armed transports, the *Recherche* and the *Espérance*, left Brest on September 28, 1791, under the command of General d'Entre-casteaux. En route to Cape of Good Hope, this officer learned that a report of Commodore Hunter described the Admiralty Islands as the probable site of the shipwreck of La Pérouse.

The two transports sailed directly for this archipelago, but they were poor sailers opposed by unfavorable weather and did not arrive there until July 28, 1792. Their search was fruitless. There was no evidence that any European ship had been lost in these waters. D'Entrecasteaux followed the orders which he had been given. Some first-class scientific treatises, published by Roussel and Labillardière, were the only results achieved from a vast outlay of money and manpower. The personnel of the expedition came off worse than ever before had been the case. Three commanding officers died—d'Entrecasteaux, Huon de Kermadec, and d'Auribeau—and with them a good part of the crew. Finally, upon their arrival at Java, the two ships were confiscated by the Dutch authorities. What was most remarkable about this voyage is that both consorts passed right by the island they were looking for, Vanikoro, the site of the disaster of La Pérouse, where they certainly would have found recent traces of the wreck and perhaps some survivors.

From this time until 1825, no attempt was made to renew the search. The *Uranie* and the *Coquille*, which were sent into the South Seas after the Restoration, did not have this objective. It was not until the Ministry received Captain d'Urville's proposal toward the end of 1825 that any thought was given to renewing the search. At that time there was a rumor in France of a whaler who claimed to have seen a cross of St. Louis[2] and some medals in the hands of the savages in New Caledonia and the Louisiade Archipelago. The details of the report seemed to be accurate and specific. The Minister of the Navy took the matter into consideration. M. d'Urville was ordered to investigate the accuracy of the reports and to attempt a solution of the mystery. The name of his ship, the *Coquille*, was changed to the *Astrolabe*.

The *Astrolabe* left France with very doubtful information, but some

---

[2] The Order of St. Louis was founded by Louis XIV in 1693 for military merit.

valuable evidence was available along her course. His voyage to Port Jackson [Sydney, Australia], far from revealing nothing to him, led d'Urville to reject the rumors drifting about in France. At Tongatabu he had the good fortune to learn from the *Tamaha*[3] that after La Pérouse left Botany Bay he stopped at Nomuka.[4] Finally, at the end of 1827, while d'Urville was stopping at Hobart, capital of Tasmania, he came upon fresh evidence. In that town, he heard of a discovery made by an Englishman, Captain Dillon, concerning which he collected the following information.

A veteran navigator, Dillon had been sailing the Pacific Ocean on merchant ships for twenty years when, on May 15, 1826, as captain of the *Saint Patrick* en route from Valparaiso to Bengal, he passed near Tikopia,[5] in the vicinity of the Fiji Islands. In the canoes which came out to the ship were two men whom he had left on the island thirteen years earlier, Bushard, a Prussian, and Joe, a lascar. Coming on board, Joe did some business with the crew and sold the armorer, among other things, a silver sword hilt engraved with an inscription. Questioned on this matter, the lascar replied that the hilt, as well as some other articles of European manufacture which were on Tikopia, came from a neighboring island named Vanikoro, where two large ships had been wrecked some time ago. According to Dillon, the lascar claimed that he had sailed to Vanikoro six years earlier and had seen two old men who had been sailors on the lost ships. He added that the wreckage was still there and that some of it could be salvaged.

From this account, Dillon concluded that the two ships were those of La Pérouse. He persuaded Bushard to go to Vanikoro with him, but on this occasion calms and currents prevented him from finding the place. When he arrived at Calcutta, he made his views known to the East India Company and to the Asiatic Society[6] in an official report which was more detailed and more precise than the account later published.

---

[3] The governing council.—Valentin

[4] In the Tonga Islands.

[5] Several hundred miles northwest of Fiji and one hundred fifty miles east-southeast of Vanikoro.

[6] The Royal Asiatic Society of Bengal was founded in 1784 to promote the study of oriental cultures.

"Upon examining the hilt," Dillon stated, "I believed that I could make out the initials of the name of La Pérouse. This led me to form certain conjectures and to pursue my questioning as far as possible. Through my interpreters, Bushard and the lascar, I interrogated several natives to determine how their neighbors had been able to obtain all the iron and silver objects which they had. They informed me that the natives of Vanikoro used to tell how, many years earlier, two large ships had come to their islands, and how they had dropped anchor, one at Vanu Island and the other at nearby Paiu Island. A few days later and before they had established contact with the natives, a storm arose and drove the two ships aground. The one anchored at Vanu struck upon the rocks. Armed with clubs, spears, and bows, the natives then massed along the shore and discharged several arrows against the ship. The crew replied with cannon fire and killed a number of the savages. As the waves continued to batter the ship against the rocks, she soon began to go to pieces. Some members of the crew leaped into the boats and were blown ashore where the natives killed them as soon as they landed; others swam ashore only to meet the fate of their companions, so that not a single man was left alive.

"The vessel which ran aground at Paiu came to rest upon a sandy beach. The natives attacked this ship with bows and arrows just as they had the other, but her crew were prudent enough not to fire back. Instead, they showed their assailants peace offerings of hatchets, glass beads, and other gewgaws, whereupon hostilities were ended. As soon as the wind had died down somewhat, an old man left the shore in a canoe and boarded the ship. He was one of the local chiefs. They received him with kindness and offered him presents, which he accepted. Returning to land, he pacified his people and told them that the men on the ship were good and friendly. At this, several natives proceeded to come aboard, where presents were offered to all of them. Before long they returned to give the crew yams, poultry, bananas, coconuts, and pigs, thus establishing confidence on both sides.

"The crew were forced to abandon ship. When the white men went ashore, they brought with them a large part of their supplies. They remained on the island for some time and built a small vessel from the wreckage of the large one. As soon as the small ship was ready to set sail, it left with as many men as it could conveniently carry, well supplied by the natives with fresh food. The commander promised the men remaining on the island that he would return for them without delay and at the same time bring gifts for the natives. The islanders, however, never heard anything more of the small craft nor of those who sailed in it. The mariners who were left on the island were distributed among the different chiefs with whom they remained as long as they lived. They had kept some of the muskets and powder, and these articles placed them in a position to render considerable service to their friends in battles with natives on neighboring islands.

"The Prussian had never ventured to sail to Mallicolo (Vanikoro) with the natives; the lascar, however, had gone there once or twice. He claimed that at Paiu he had seen two Europeans who spoke the native language and that he had conversed with them. They were old men, who told him that they had been shipwrecked a number of years ago in one of the vessels, the remains of which they showed him. They told him also that no ship had touched at the islands of Vanikoro since their arrival and that most of their shipmates had died, but because they had been scattered among the various islands, they had no exact way of determining how many were still alive."

The East India Company was eager to collect all the information possible about a man who had served science with so much devotion and who had sacrificed himself to promote its progress. They decided to send one of their ships, the *Research*, under Dillon's command, to explore the islands of Vanikoro in order to make certain that the French captain had been shipwrecked on those shores. They did everything possible to make the expedition a scientific success. Dr. Tytler, the author of several well-known works, was the expedition's surgeon, naturalist, and historian. His salary was considerable, as was Dillon's, since the company was sparing no expense. They appropriated two thousand rupees just for the purchase of goods to be distributed as gifts among the natives of Vanikoro. Going even further, they brought on the *Research* a French representative who would officially verify the findings. This was a certain M. Chagneau, at that time employed at Chandernagor.

The *Research* set sail on January 23, 1827. They had been at sea only a few days when Dr. Tytler and Captain Dillon had a violent quarrel. It was so vehement that when they reached Hobart the doctor brought charges against the captain before a military court. Dillon was found guilty, sentenced to two months' imprisonment, and fined £50. In addition, he was required to post bond of £400 against his future conduct. Since the penalty imposed upon Dillon would delay the expedition, an attempt was made to replace him, but the crafty mariner had not revealed the position of Vanikoro to anyone, and under another commander the expedition would probably have failed. Part of his sentence, therefore, had to be suspended. Dillon was required to pay the fine and post the bond, but he was spared the imprisonment.

Upon the conclusion of this unfortunate affair, the *Research* left Hobart on May 20 and arrived at Sydney on June 3, for a brief stop. They dropped anchor at Korora-Reka in Bay of Islands on July 1. From there they went to Tongatabu, thence to Rotuma and to Tikopia. At the last island they picked up a native named Ratia, who was to serve as guide and interpreter. They also acquired there a number of objects from the wrecked ships. The *Research* finally reached Vanikoro on the 7th, and after six days spent in exploring for an anchorage, they dropped anchor in the little harbor of Ocili, in East Bay.

As soon as Dillon landed here, he set to work collecting all the relics of the shipwreck which were left on the island. Thanks to his lavishness with hardware, cloth, and glass beads, he managed to gather a surprisingly large amount. Most of the material consisted of hooks, bolts, chain links, and other ironware; pulley wheels, cooking pots, spoons, trays, and copper funnels; various parts of astronomical instruments and cooking utensils. One of the most important objects was a large bronze bell, one foot in diameter. On one side it had a crucifix between two figures, and on the other side a sun with rays; in the center it bore the legend: "Bazin made me." Inquiries made in France showed that these marks were used at the Brest navy yard around 1785. On the western reefs they also recovered four bronze swivel guns, an eighteen-pound cannonball, a Spanish dollar, pieces of cutglass, porcelain, earthenware, bottles and glasses, and various other iron, copper, and lead objects.

An even more valuable find was a fir plank four feet long and fourteen inches wide, decorated with a fleur-de-lis and various other carvings. When returned to France, this ornament was recognized as a fragment of the taffrail of one of La Pérouse's ships. At Vanikoro the natives had made it into a door panel. A millstone which had been part of a handmill was found in the same enclosure.

The natives, moreover, did not deny that the shipwreck had occurred. Each told the story in his own way, and the captain of the *Research* quoted various versions which he heard. The most detailed and probably the most accurate, that of Valie, the second *aligui* (chief) of Vanu, is given below.

"A long time ago," declared the chief, "the inhabitants of this island came out of their cabins in the morning to see half of a ship on the reef opposite Paiu. It remained there until about noon when the sea finally hammered it to pieces. Large sections of debris drifted along the shore. During the night the ship had been driven upon the reef by a frightful hurricane which broke a great number of our fruit trees. We had not seen the ship the day before. Four men escaped from it and reached land nearby. We were going to kill them, when they gave some gift to our chief, who saved their lives. They remained with us a short time, and then they left to join their companions at Paiu. There they built a small ship in which they sailed away. None of those four men was a chief, but they were all of lesser rank. The objects which we are selling come from a vessel which grounded on the reef at low tide. Our people made a practice of diving there and bringing up whatever they could. Much of the wreckage came to shore, and we removed a number of things from it. Nothing is being recovered from the vessel any longer because the hull rotted away and disappeared in the sea. We did not kill any of this ship's crew, but along the shore we found a number of bodies whose arms and legs had been mutilated by the sharks. During that same night, another vessel ran upon a reef and foundered near Vanu. There were several survivors. They built a small ship and left five moons before the big ship disappeared. While they were building the small ship, they set up a stout stockade around their place as defense against attack by the islanders. The latter, for their part, feared the strangers, so that there was little communication between the two sides. The white men were in the habit of looking at the sun through certain objects, which I can neither describe nor show since we have none of them in our possession. Two white men remained behind after their companions left. One was a chief, the other his servant. The former died about three years ago. Half a year later the chief of the district in which the other white man lived was forced to flee from the island, and the white man left with him. The district which they quit was called Paukori, but we do not know what became of the tribe which lived there at that time. The only white men whom the islanders have ever seen were first those who were shipwrecked and now those whom we see today."

Dillon made several trips into the island without being troubled by the natives in any way, since he had won them over by his generosity. His observations, recorded in his report, are of no special interest. A so-called map of Vanikoro, drawn by him, is very inaccurate and incomplete.

At the beginning of October, fearing that the east winds would not permit him to remain in the bay, he successfully negotiated the dangerous west channel and dropped anchor in the quiet waters of Manevai Bay, staying there for three days. Then he left by the north channel and sailed before the wind toward Tubua [Utupua] and Nitendi [Ndeni or Santa Cruz Island], and then to New Zealand. After a rather long stop, he crossed over to Sydney and from there set sail for Calcutta, where he arrived April 7, 1828. Generously paid for his efforts, he obtained the company's permission to go to France with the evidence of his discovery. He received a hero's welcome in Paris and was presented to King Charles X, who bestowed the cross of the Legion of Honor upon him, ten thousand francs to defray the cost of his voyage, and a pension of four thousand francs. In addition, the king promised him that all of the objects which he had collected would be placed in a cenotaph to be erected for this purpose in one of the halls of the naval museum which was being established under the name of the Dauphin Museum.[7]

---

[7] This promise was carried out. The articles recovered from the wreckage were arranged in the form of a pyramid at the entrance of the naval museum at the Louvre, as a monument intended to perpetuate the memory of the glory and the tragedy of Admiral La Pérouse. The pyramid contains, among other objects, four small cannon

D'Urville learned of Dillon's work on December 20, 1827, at Hobart, where some newspapers had reported briefly on his expedition.

Dillon had spoken of Tikopia and of Vanikoro, but without giving their exact positions. That was his secret. It was therefore necessary to make a systematic search for the island, a problem which was not beyond d'Urville's ability to solve. Penetrating Dillon's evasiveness, he saw that Tikopia was the old Barwel Island of the English maps and that Vanikoro had to be one of the islands located southeast of Santa Cruz or the group, discovered by Bligh, north of the New Hebrides. From then on his plan was set. He decided to find Tikopia, or Barwel, and there to learn from the natives what island was the site of the shipwreck.

While Captain d'Urville was preparing to depart, two letters from Dillon arrived in Hobart; completely contradictory, one stated that he was postponing his voyage because of a so-called monsoon, and the other announced that he had just made some valuable discoveries. Although these puzzling reports must have compounded the French commander's confusion, they in no way lessened his determination.

The *Astrolabe* set sail on January 6, 1828. They sighted Norfolk Island and the volcanic Matthew Island, then the islands of Fataka [Mitre] and Anuda [Cherry], and on February 10 they appeared off Tikopia. The corvette had scarcely come into view of the island when she was greeted by a canoe bearing the Prussian, Bushard, who had accompanied Dillon to Vanikoro. He confirmed Dillon's account of his voyage and thus put an end to Captain d'Urville's long-standing uncertainty. To have obtained this evidence was in itself a great achievement, but it was still necessary to complete the mission with personal observation. It was also necessary for the expedition to pay its last respects to those who had given their lives for the advancement of science and navigation.

Some of the officers and naturalists went ashore at Tikopia and received a welcome in a native council hall to which Bushard had conducted them. This individual had promised to guide the *Astrolabe* to Vanikoro provided his wife, a young New Zealander, could accompany him on the trip, but

---

set in like pilasters, part of a silver ladle, several swivel guns, and two bells, the larger of which is at the top and the smaller at the bottom of the pile.—Valentin

a short time later he withdrew his promise. One of the excuses offered in justification for his refusal was the unhealthiness of Vanikoro.

Proposals made to the natives met with the same response. When Joe the lascar was requested to serve as guide, he was as unwilling as the others. He claimed that he had never told Captain Dillon that he had been to Vanikoro.

As a result, Captain d'Urville had to be satisfied with taking two Englishmen who had been on Tikopia for nine months. One of them, who had a fair command of the native language, could serve as interpreter. Five Tikopians involuntarily accompanied the French on their voyage. These had been inadvertently left on board the ship after all the canoes had departed.

Captain d'Urville sailed directly to Vanikoro, the position of which he had determined despite Dillon's secretiveness. Delayed by calms on the way, he did not reach the island until the 14th. He sailed along its reef, sent a boat out to explore for the anchorage, and took advantage of contrary northwest winds to search for Tumako, which Quiros reported near Santa Cruz but which was never seen again. He cruised about for three days without finding this island, then he turned back toward Vanikoro and dropped anchor on the 21st in the small, dangerous roadstead of Ocili, where the *Research* had anchored, and which the villagers of Manevai had pointed out to the expedition.

After the *Astrolabe* was properly moored, M. d'Urville's first task was to win over the natives with the help of some presents. On any other occasion the goods which were offered to them would have been regarded by the islanders as fabulous, but Dillon had spoiled them with his lavishness, and everything they received left them cold. The sight of their defiant attitude and ill will should have warned the French to take precautions and cleverly to infuse them with a sense of fear. As a matter of fact, the islanders later claimed that they had been informed that the French were fellow countrymen of those who had been shipwrecked and that they were undoubtedly coming to take revenge for the tragedy which had taken place on these shores.

All of these obstacles in no way disheartened M. d'Urville, and boats were sent out under the *Astrolabe*'s officers to make a reconnaissance of the island. As they proceeded along the coast they were to collect remnants of the wreckage and native reports of the disaster, and at the same time they were to prepare a chart of the island and to note its natural phenomena. Thus all of their objectives would be accomplished simultaneously.

The first party, commanded by M. Gressien, brought back only a small amount of relatively insignificant wreckage. This party obtained no information, for in response to all their questions, the natives maintained complete silence or gave evasive answers. Fear had evidently made them all adopt an absolutely negative attitude to everything relating to the wreck of the frigates. When one of them, more talkative than the rest and more susceptible to presents, prepared to give some information, his neighbors immediately expressed their displeasure and dismay by surrounding him and by inducing him to be silent or forcing him to leave.

The second party, under M. Jacquinot,[8] at first experienced similar setbacks. At Vanu, the coming of the French alarmed the village's small population. The women seized their children and their most precious possessions and fled into the woods. Only the men approached the boat, and their attitude expressed anxiety and fear. When questioned, they denied everything, but they finally admitted that for a long time they had in their possession some skulls of *maras* (their name for Europeans), but later had thrown them into the sea.

The chief, Valie, mentioned by Dillon, was the only one who showed that he was trustworthy and sincere. On several occasions he was on the verge of telling the whole story, but his fellow islanders' threats stopped him. At Nama there was the same silence, the same dissembling. At first, regardless of what was offered to them, the natives refused to point out the site of the shipwreck, but when M. Jacquinot began to unroll before their eyes a piece of red cloth, the sight of this material had such an exciting effect upon one of the savages that he immediately leaped into the boat, gesturing that he would lead them to the desired place if they gave him

---

[8] Charles Hector Jacquinot, an officer on the *Astrolabe* during d'Urville's first voyage, became captain of the *Zelée*, which sailed with the *Astrolabe* under the command of d'Urville on his second voyage (1837–1840).

the precious piece of cloth. The deal was promptly closed, and M. Jacquinot soon arrived at the reef where the disaster had taken place.

The chain of reefs which encircles Vanikoro at a distance of two or three miles from shore turns landward in front of Paiu and Ambi, where it is scarcely more than a mile from land. There, in a kind of pass between the breakers, the native indicated that the boat should stop as he gestured toward the bottom of the water. The Frenchmen looked down, and at a depth of twelve to fifteen feet, they made out anchors, cannon, shot, and lead bars strewn about and encrusted with coral. This sight ended their doubts—one of La Pérouse's ships was lost upon the rocks of this reef.

All the wood, destroyed by the action of the weather and the waves, had disappeared; the metal, being more durable and resistant, was all that remained. The location of the anchors indicated that four of them had gone down with the ship, while the other two could have been holding the ship. Finally, the hydrographical features of the place indicated that the ship had entered this pass in order to get behind the line of breakers, that she had run aground in the channel and had been unable to disengage. Some of the natives stated that it was from this ship that the crew had come to Paiu where they built a small craft, while the other ship had run aground outside of the reef and had been completely engulfed.

As soon as he arrived at the site of the wreck, M. Jacquinot immediately attempted to raise some of the remains. A sling was fastened to an anchor, but it was so firmly fixed in the bottom that the operation had to be abandoned to avoid jeopardizing the boat. Later, M. Guilbert was more fortunate. When he was ordered to recover what was left of the wreckage, his operation was so strenuous that it cracked the stern of the longboat, but he succeeded in tearing from the coral crust covering the sea's bottom an eighteen-hundred-pound anchor and a short, cast iron cannon which was heavily corroded and caked with a layer two inches thick. A brass swivel gun, a copper blunderbuss, a pig of iron, and a lead bar—this is what they salvaged after forty years.

After seeing the remains brought back by the longboat, no one doubted any longer that these objects had belonged to La Pérouse's frigates. Nevertheless, to forestall any charge that he had given in to wishful thinking, M. d'Urville assembled all the members of his staff for their opinion. Each one declared that in his mind it was now an established fact that La Pérouse had been wrecked on Vanikoro.

Unfavorable conditions in the harbor of Ocili were damaging the *Astrolabe*. The swell was weakening the cables and threatening to run her against the steep rocks along the shore, where she would have gone down in fifteen fathoms of water. The commander decided to change his position. By warping the ship, he moved into Manevai Bay, a huge, perfectly protected harbor. There the people they met were more sociable. The natives, who were enemies of the people of Tonnevai, ran on board the *Astrolabe*. The chiefs greeted the captain in their own manner, by kissing the backs of their hands, and one of them, the senior chief and high priest of Manevai, whose name was Moembe, claimed to be the captain's special friend. About fifty years of age, he was small in stature, ugly even among his own people, continually good-natured, with a gentle personality, a peaceful disposition, and dignified, courteous manners. Moembe became M. d'Urville's friend and often came to visit him. He answered d'Urville's questions to the best of his ability, asked none, patiently awaited whatever presents were given to him, and accepted them with gratitude.

Nelo, the chief of Tevai, behaved in quite a different manner. With his never-ending demands, his disagreeable, unobliging disposition, he was a perfect ingrate, who followed every present with a request for more. One day this tiresome behavior almost resulted in a serious disagreement. Accompanied by several unarmed officers, Captain d'Urville had gone to visit Nelo at Tevai. Old Nelo, surly as ever, received his visitors in the *house of the spirits*, where he was surrounded by his warriors armed with bows and arrows. At first he complained in his usual way that no one had given him any presents. He repeatedly asked for hatchets, saying that *Pita* (Captain Peter Dillon) had given him "much, much." To this the French commander answered that if Nelo sent fresh food on board, pigs in particular, he would receive hatchets. He even specified that three hatchets would be paid for one pig, a price to which Nelo agreed. When the pigs did not appear, the commander attempted to return to his ship, but the savages adopted such a threatening attitude that it seemed imprudent for unarmed men to get involved with them. To avoid a disaster, a ruse was tried. M. d'Urville offered the chief a large hatchet and a fine necklace, saying that these were to be credited to his account against the pigs which had been promised. Then he rose and left. Surprised and fascinated by the gift, Nelo did not oppose his departure. The captain thought himself fortunate to have escaped this type of ambush so cheaply.

The scientific work, however, went on apace. Gaimard, the naturalist, had received permission from the commander to land by himself on the western part of the island. Prudence, however, required him to take a companion, an Englishman named Hamilton, who spoke the Vanikoran language indifferently. The inhabitants of Nama seemed fascinated at the sight of these strangers, but during the five days that M. Gaimard and the Englishman were with them, they showed that they were not always obliging and hospitable. This expedition, perilous and meritorious as it was, produced no useful results and, at the end of five days, the naturalist returned with a high fever, having had every imaginable difficulty defending himself against the angry wild men. It was impossible to establish mutual trust, and even the village of Nama was closed to the French explorer.

After receiving his associates' opinion on the remains of La Pérouse's wreck, Captain d'Urville informed them of a project which he had formed a long time ago. This was the erection of a monument to commemorate their countrymen who had given their lives for science, until such time as France, in keeping with her dignity as a great power, could dedicate a more lasting memorial. This proposal met an enthusiastic reception, with everyone wishing to participate in the erection of the cenotaph.

Since it was impossible to set it up at Paiu, the exact site of the disaster, the place selected was a cluster of mangroves growing on the reef which partly surrounded the anchorage at Manevai. The monument was built in the shape of a cube, measuring six feet on each side, surmounted by a four-sided pyramid of the same dimensions. The bulk of the structure consisted of layers of coral contained by heavy piles driven into the ground, and the top was covered with a small cap of planks purchased in New Zealand. To protect the cenotaph from the covetousness of the savages, the French were careful not to use any nails or iron bands. Once begun, the work on the memorial progressed rapidly, despite the tasks on shipboard and the difficulties experienced by the new *Astrolabe* in the locale which was so fatal for the old one.

The fever of Gaimard, the naturalist, had grown worse. Even the captain, the night before he went to visit the place where the shipwrecked men had built their small craft, was seized by severe and dangerous attacks of fever. Since the weather, which had been dry, suddenly turned rainy and unhealthy, the fever became epidemic and struck several members of the crew in succession.

Nevertheless, the monument was completed on March 14 and was dedicated on the same day, in the presence of members of the crew who had landed on the reef. A detachment of ten armed men marched around the cenotaph three times in the midst of a solemn and respectful silence, and then they saluted the dead with three salvoes of their muskets while the ship fired a twenty-one gun salute which resounded through the mountains of Vanikoro. Forty years before, these very mountains probably echoed with the cries of our countrymen dying under the blows of the savages. Mourning became this tragic island, mourning in this act of dedication, mourning in the dismal, frightening plight of the expedition. The fever had by then confined half of the *Astrolabe*'s crew to their hammocks and seemed to be threatening the other half. The corvette would be short-handed while passing through the difficult and dangerous channels. A few more days there and the cenotaph on the reef would be able to memorialize two disasters. Captain d'Urville felt the immediate presence of danger. Although he too had been attacked by the fever, he still had the strength to give the necessary orders for moving the ship out of this dreaded place. Every exertion increased the number of the sick. Finally, on March 17, they made an all-out effort. Here is M. d'Urville's own account of this critical operation.

"Forty men were incapacitated, and if we let that day (March 17) pass without moving, tomorrow perhaps it would be too late to think of leaving Vanikoro. Consequently, I had decided to make one final effort. At six o'clock in the morning we would weigh anchors and warp the ship out, a tedious and difficult operation in view of the fact that the rope, cable, and hawser were twisted around each other and we had few men on deck.

"At eight o'clock, while we were in the middle of this operation, I was most astonished to see about half a dozen Tevai canoes coming toward us, especially when three or four natives of Manevai who were on board did not seem to be at all frightened at their approach, even though they had told me that the people of Tevai were their mortal enemies. I expressed my surprise to the men from Manevai, but they merely laughed evasively, saying that they had made peace with Tevai and that these men were bringing me coconuts. I soon saw that the new arrivals had only their bows and arrows, which appeared in a high state of readiness. Two or three of them came on board with a very determined air and went over to the main hatch to look into the spar-deck and see for themselves how many men were sick. At the same time their demoniacal faces broke out into a look of malevolent satisfaction. Meanwhile, some members of the crew brought my attention to the fact that two or three Manevai men who were on board had been engaged in this same kind of spying for three or four days. M. Gressien had been watching their movements since morning, and he believed that he had seen the warriors of both tribes meet on the beach for a lengthy conference.

"These activities indicated their treacherous inclination, and I decided that we were in imminent danger. I immediately ordered the natives to leave the corvette and get into their canoes. They had the audacity to look at me fiercely and menacingly, as if to dare me to enforce my order. I simply had the arms locker, which we usually were careful to keep closed, opened wide; then, with a stern expression, with one hand I directed the attention of the savages to the weapons and with the other I pointed to their canoes. The sight of twenty shining muskets, the power of which they understood, gave them a start, and we were soon rid of their presence.

"It is essential to remember that these uncivilized men can be restrained simply by their fear of firearms. The European can accomplish more by this than by actually firing. The sight of a single pistol can put twenty savages to flight, while they have been known to throw themselves like wild beasts upon a detachment which had just fired upon them.

"Nevertheless, we had now severed relations, as it were, with these savages, and our departure had become more imperative than ever. I therefore urged the crew to take courage and redouble their efforts while

I hastened the time of getting under way as much as my feeble means permitted. Weak as they were, even the sick men lent a hand in the work, and we were finally able to drop an anchor to the east in thirty fathoms of water. Although the anchor fouled, we were quite happy that it finally took hold.

"This was our precarious position when, on March 17, 1828, at 11:15 A.M., the *Astrolabe* spread her sails and made her great effort to leave Vanikoro. At first we hauled as close to the wind as possible, with a fairly strong east-southeast breeze. Then we let her bear down on the pass, but at the very moment when we were entering the most dangerous section of the passage where it is thick with rocks, an unexpected squall closed in on us, reducing visibility to a radius of less than five hundred feet.

"Overcome by the fever, I had scarcely enough strength to direct the handling of the ship, and my weakened eyes were unable to focus on the foaming waves which whitened both sides of the pass. I was ably assisted, however, by the officers, especially by M. Gressien, whom I had made responsible for steering the ship. He served as the pilot and acted with so much coolness, prudence, and skill that the corvette negotiated the narrow and dangerous pass and safely reached the open water. It was here that the fate of the expedition was at stake, and the slightest false move would have thrown the corvette upon the rocks with no possibility of saving her. And so, despite our exhausted condition, after several anxious minutes when we saw that we had cleared the reefs of this ill-fated island, all of us experienced a surge of joy similar to that felt by a prisoner who has escaped the horrors of the most inhuman captivity. Gentle hope came to revive our shattered spirits, and our thoughts turned once again to the shores of our native land, across the five or six thousand leagues separating us from home."

Although this expedition had had its share of misfortune, it nevertheless produced results of scientific value; some useful work was accomplished, and important observations were made. M. Gressien drew an exact and complete map of the entire island, delineating its shoreline, reefs, and terrain features in great detail. The map produced by his arduous efforts is one of the masterpieces of the voyage. Unknown until recently, Vanikoro is now one of the most accurately described spots in the Pacific Ocean. The island's natural phenomena were studied, and specimens were collected which are now on display in the museum. In addition to this research, useful and basic as it was, the expedition accomplished its special objective, tracing the shipwreck of La Pérouse. M. d'Urville carried this investigation to its end, and his account is worth quoting because of its unusual and factual character.

"From the moment of our arrival," wrote d'Urville, "the Vanikoro Islanders, naturally as fierce and aggressive as all Melanesian savages, apparently adopted an absolutely negative attitude in regard to the disaster, or else they were sure to answer our questions with nothing but evasions such as 'I don't know,' 'I didn't see it,' 'That happened a long time ago,' 'That's what we heard our fathers say,' etc. It was obvious that their conduct toward the unfortunate men who escaped from the shipwreck was less than hospitable. No doubt they feared we had come for vengeance, especially when they had learned from the English and from other natives that we were of the same nationality as the *maras*. However, when they came to know that we had no hostile intention and when they saw how generously we offered them our friendship and gifts, their fear lessened somewhat; some of them became more talkative and more willing to answer the questions which I never stopped asking. I preferred to deal with the old men because they had witnessed the tragic events, and with the younger men who seemed to have quicker minds and better memories and were, therefore, more likely to retain what they had heard their fathers tell them.

"In my report I have given the results of these various conversations, and it will be seen that among the former stand out Yaliko, chief of Vanikoro village; a very old chief of Manevai; and Moembe, chief priest of the same village. In the other group, the most important were Tangaloa and Kava-Liki, very intelligent young chiefs who proudly described themselves as the offspring of a father from Tikopia and a Vanikoro mother, parentage which made them part Polynesian. By comparing, analyzing, and evaluating their various accounts, the following version has been adopted as the nearest to the truth.

"After a very dark night, during which there was a gale from the southeast, suddenly at dawn the natives sighted a huge canoe grounded upon the reefs south of the island, opposite the Tanema district. She was soon destroyed by the waves, disappearing without a trace, so that it was impossible to salvage anything. Only a small number of men on board were able to escape in a boat and reach land. On the morning of the following day, the savages saw a second canoe, similar to the first one, grounded in front of Paiu. In the lee of the island, this vessel was less strained by wind and sea. Furthermore, she was resting on an even bottom in twelve to fifteen feet of water and, therefore, remained in place for a long time without disintegrating. The strangers who were on board her landed at Paiu, where they and the survivors of the other ship established a base and immediately went to work building a small craft from the remains of the ship which had not foundered.

"The French, whom the natives called *maras*, were, so they said, always respected by the islanders, who habitually kissed their hands when they approached them—a custom which they practiced often on the officers of the *Astrolabe* during their stay at the island. Nevertheless, there were frequent quarrels, and in the course of one of these the natives lost several warriors, including three chiefs, and some of the French were killed. Finally, after working six or seven moons, they finished the small craft. According to the opinion of most, all of the strangers left the island. Some claimed that two of the *maras* remained behind, but they did not live long. On this point there was little doubt, all agreeing that it was impossible for any Frenchman to be still living either on Vanikoro or on Tikopia, or even on Nitendi or any neighboring island. As for the skulls of the unfortunate Frenchmen who died at the hands of these savages, these had probably been preserved for a long time as trophies of their victory, but if they still had them at the time of our arrival, they most likely hurried to hide them where we would have no chance of finding them.

"Everything leads us to believe that after La Pérouse visited the Friendly Islands and completed his reconnaissance of New Caledonia, he headed north on a course for the Santa Cruz Islands, as his instructions directed him to do and as he himself states in his last report to the Minister of the Navy. As he neared these islands, he undoubtedly believed that he could continue on his course during the night, as he had so often done, when he suddenly came upon the terrible reefs of Vanikoro, the very existence of which was unknown. It was probably the leading frigate (the objects recovered by Dillon indicate that this was the *Boussole*) which struck the rocks and became immovable, while the other one had time to turn up into the wind and regain the open sea. The horrible prospect of leaving their friends, perhaps their commander, to the mercies of a savage tribe was too much for those who had avoided the first hazard. Incapable of sailing away from this tragic island, they had to make every effort to rescue their countrymen from the fate which was threatening them. This, we are certain, was the reason for the loss of the second ship. The configuration of the shoreline where this vessel stranded gives added weight to this opinion, for at first glance it would seem possible to find a passage through the reefs. The Frenchmen on the second ship, therefore, may have tried to get beyond the rocks by passing through an opening in the reef and did not discover their mistake until they too were hopelessly grounded.

"Although no document has been found to provide direct positive proof that these remains actually came from the La Pérouse expedition, I do not think that there can be the slightest doubt about it. As a matter of fact, the information which I obtained from the natives is perfectly consistent in all essential respects with that obtained by Dillon. Neither of us could have been influenced by the other, since I did not learn of his report to the French government until two months after I had sent mine to the Ministry. These statements are, therefore, perfectly authentic. They prove that two large ships were destroyed about forty years ago on the reefs of Vanikoro and that they had a large complement on board; the natives even remembered that they flew a white banner. All this, together with the cannon and swivel guns which were recovered, proves that these were warships. Furthermore, it is a known fact that for a long time before and after this period the only ships lost in these waters were La Pérouse's frigates and the *Pandora*, commanded by Edwards,[9] which

---

[9] Captain Edward Edwards of the *Pandora* discovered Rotuma Island in 1791. He had been sent to the South Seas to apprehend the mutineers of the *Bounty*. After arresting several of them at Tahiti, he was on his way back when the *Pandora* was wrecked. The survivors made their way in the boats to Timor, and Edwards later turned in a report of his voyage to the Admiralty.

was wrecked on the reefs of Torres Strait. Moreover, the nature of some of the material recovered from the wreck proves that the ships were engaged in a mission of an unusual kind. Finally, the only piece of wood brought back by Dillon was found to have the same designs as those carved on the *Boussole*'s stern. Such an accumulation of evidence ought to be sufficient to dispel all doubt!

"Since I undoubtedly will be called upon to express my opinion regarding the probable course followed by the French after leaving Vanikoro, I will state that, as I see it, they must have steered for New Ireland on a course toward the Moluccas or the Philippines, following the same route as Carteret or Bougainville. For this was the only course which offered some chance of success to a vessel as small and as poorly equipped as that built at Vanikoro must have been, since we must also assume that the Frenchmen had been greatly weakened by fever and by the attacks of the natives.

"I will go even further and declare that the western coast of the Solomon Islands is where some trace of their journey will later be found."[10]

Captain d'Urville's last statement was based on so reasonable an inference that when he left Vanikoro he wanted to explore the Solomon Islands in order, if possible, to follow in the tracks of the Frenchmen. However, the desperate condition of his crew forced him to sail straight for the Mariana Islands, the only stop where the sick could expect some relief.

When the news of Dillon's discoveries first arrived in France, it was feared that Captain d'Urville, who had already departed on his expedition, would be unable to make use of this information to locate the site of the wreck. To resolve this problem, the Minister of the Navy ordered M. le Goarant, commander of the corvette *Bayonnaise*, then stationed on the

[10] After he had written these lines, Captain d'Urville made another voyage around the world. He moved much farther toward the south pole than any of those who had preceded him into that dangerous region, and he discovered new territories which he named Louis-Philippe Land, Amelia Land, etc. By his skill and courage, he was able to avoid the dangers which often surrounded him, but a horrible death awaited him after he landed in France. After winning fame and honorable retirement, the illustrious navigator perished in the tragic Paris–Versailles railway accident of May 8, 1842.—Valentin

west coast of America, to sail for Tikopia and Vanikoro, where he was to engage in the investigation required to determine where La Pérouse was shipwrecked.

M. le Goarant left Valparaiso on February 8, 1828, and followed a course taking him to the Hawaiian Islands, Fanning, Sydney, Phoenix, Rotuma, and Tikopia. At the last place, he found Bushard the Prussian and Joe the lascar. The former remained deaf to all propositions that he sail with them, but Joe, who had just lost his wife, was more obliging and came on board the *Bayonnaise*. The corvette appeared before Vanikoro on June 3 and, according to the captain's report, spent more than twelve days there without mooring anywhere. This spared her from the island's fevers, but her reconnaissance by sail produced nothing of value for geography or science; the question of La Pérouse's wreck, moreover, remained exactly where Captain d'Urville had left it. It was unfortunate that the *Bayonnaise*, with a crew twice that of the *Astrolabe*, did not send a strong landing party into Paiu, where they could have made excavations which might well have verified the presence of the French. The most remarkable event which occurred while the *Bayonnaise* was off Vanikoro was the discovery by one of her boats of the cenotaph which had been erected a short time before by the sailors of the *Astrolabe*. Far from destroying the monument, the natives regarded it with veneration, and they almost prevented the newcomers from nailing on a medal attesting the visit of the *Bayonnaise*. Thus, there is reason to expect this memorial to last as long as the fragile material of which it was made.

No doubt other navigators have seen Vanikoro since the expeditions of d'Urville and le Goarant, for the naval museum has received a tree trunk from this island with the date 1788 on it, carved, it would seem, by one of the survivors of the wreck. Nevertheless, since we have no information on the authenticity and origin of this unusual object, no discussion of it is included in this account which is limited to the exact, official record.

INDEX

Voyages and Adventures of La Pérouse *has been set in Monotype Walbaum, a typeface originally produced by Justus Erich Walbaum of Germany around the year 1800 and modeled after late eighteenth-century designs of the French typefounder Firmin Didot. Less severely precise than its French prototypes, Walbaum has been alternately criticized and admired for the slight irregularities of its cut.*

Composed by William Clowes and Sons Ltd. Printed offset on 60 lb. Warren's Olde Style by Universal Lithographers, Inc. Bound in GSB natural finish fabrics by L. H. Jenkins, Inc.

Designed by James Wageman, Acorn Studio